Praise for *Presentation Advantage*

"We live and work in a distracted world and all of us are short on time. Any successful business professional needs to have the skills and ability to captivate and grasp the attention of their audience, whether online or in front of a live audience. FranklinCovey's *Presentation Advantage* gives you the tools to be a masterful and confident presenter and helps you to gain that competitive advantage in persuading your audiences to listen and take action."

—Regina R. Testa, VP, Marketing, US GCO,
Xerox Corporation

"Effective communication is too frequently elusive. In our daily business activities we are all too often the victims of poor presentations, dull and lifeless PowerPoint decks, and impassionate messages. Few of us possess the right skillset to be truly effective communicators. From the first page, FranklinCovey's *Presentation Advantage* identifies the problem and provides a clear path and the tools of how to deliver an effective, passionate message to captivate an audience within the presentation's most critical first thirty seconds. This is a must-read for all managerial and executive level team members . . . no, for anybody who wants to be heard!"

—Paul Schwartz, President and CEO,
ThermoLift, Inc., and serial entrepreneur

"So practical! The develop-design-deliver process is practical and powerful for all sorts of commun̶i̶c̶a̶t̶i̶o̶n̶ everyday meetings to formal presentations. Using this simple model you learn how to inject passion and purpose into any conversation. Anyone looking to truly connect with an audience will treasure this book because it provides an easy, pragmatic process to become an effective communicator, an essential skill for any professional."

—Colleen Dockendorf, Vice President of Human Resources, Ryan Companies US, Inc.

"I believe one of the most common faults people have is disrespecting other people's time. Poorly planned, developed, and delivered presentations do precisely that—waste people's precious time. FranklinCovey's *Presentation Advantage* is a well-organized, comprehensive guide that steps you through the process of creating and delivering a highly effective presentation. It's a necessary and fundamental read for anyone who is involved in the presentation process."

—Michael E. Fox, President, Dainippon Screen USA

"For many, public speaking or making a presentation of any sort is one of the most terrifying experiences imaginable. This book, *Presentation Advantage*, provides an antidote to that fear. Whether you are a first-time presenter or an experienced speaker, this excellent book offers an engaging and helpful approach to improving your communication skills. Equally important, the book provides a systematic approach to preparing and giving a talk, thus making the whole process very manageable. Through the use of examples and clear explanation, the process of presentation is demystified. Reading this book was fun and confidence-building."

—Judith G. Regensteiner, Ph.D., Director of the Center for Women's Health Research, University of Colorado School of Medicine

"We've all been there, in another boring meeting or presentation, where we're looking at our smartphones and thinking about what else we need to get done instead of listening to what's being presented. We've all also been on the other side as well, trying to put together a compelling presentation that we hope captivates and adds value to our audience and beats out all the other noise and distractions. To date, most books have focused on all of the 'mechanics' of delivering a good presentation. *Presentation Advantage* does that as well, but the real value is that the book offers the secrets to make sure you're putting together and delivering an *effective* presentation. As business leaders, we want to persuade others to real action, we want to lead our audiences to do things differently, and we know we need to do that in a short amount of time . . . this book is a must-read for anyone hoping to do just that."

—Ken Ingram, SCREEN GP Americas, LLC, VP Sales and Marketing–Americas

"The key to any good message is the messenger. Without a skillful presenter, an important or powerful message will never be heard. This book can change that. In the current world of high-tech distractions and information overload, presenters have only minutes to grab attention. *Presentation Advantage* is the book that can teach you to make powerful messages that motivate others to change, which is no easy task. Powerful messaging is a skill that is often overlooked but is a true differentiator for top performance and results."

—Erica Neubert Campbell, Head of Behavior Change, Foreign and Commonwealth Office

"Learning how to effectively inform and persuade others is a business and life skill of immeasurable value. The book *Presentation Advantage* is an incredible resource that teaches presentation skills applicable in today's world of unprecedented distractions and ever-shortening attention spans. The book not only provides very practical information but it is truly a 'fun' read as well. I can't wait to share *Presentation Advantage* with my clients!"

—Gary Takacs, President and CEO, Takacs Learning Center

"Connecting with your audience is a key component of any successful presentation. FranklinCovey's *Presentation Advantage* shares proven methods for balancing the development, design, and delivery of effective presentations. In today's business culture, where storytelling and visual images are paramount for audience engagement, this program excels at teaching the significance of mastering both the style and technique of impactful presentations."

—Jennifer Day, Sr. Manager of Sales, Training, & Development, Georgia-Pacific Professional

"Complete with practical examples, a logical methodology, useful preparation tools, wit, and humor, and all the wisdom of the late Dr. Covey's writings, *Presentation Advantage* is essential reading for everyone making presentations today . . . that is, everyone!"

—Craig Escamilla, Management Instructor, Lamar University College of Business

"From a personal perspective, I wish this book had been written twenty years ago . . . my poor audiences must have been horrified. From an HR perspective, mastering these skills gives you a competitive advantage and will accelerate your career."

—Denise D. Gromley, Human Resource Director, Diamond Drugs, Inc.

"I found *Presentation Advantage* to be extremely helpful in enhancing my presentation skills—the program demonstrates many new creative techniques. I am a college professor who uses both PowerPoint and Keynote slides in my lectures. By demonstrating real-world examples of successful presentations, *Presentation Advantage* has brought my teaching to a whole new level."

—Professor Jason W. Hayes, J.D., Doane College

PRESENTATION
ADVANTAGE

PRESENTATION
ADVANTAGE

HOW TO **INFORM** AND **PERSUADE** ANY AUDIENCE

KORY KOGON,
BRECK ENGLAND,
AND JULIE SCHMIDT

A FRANKLINCOVEY BOOK

BenBella Books, Inc.

Dallas, Texas

BenBella Books, Inc.
10300 N. Central Expressway
Suite #530
Dallas, TX 75231
www.benbellabooks.com
Send feedback to feedback@benbellabooks.com

Printed in the United States of America
10 9 8 7 6 5 4 3 2 1

Library of Congress Cataloging-in-Publication Data
Kogon, Kory.
  Presentation advantage : how to inform and persuade any audience / Kory Kogon, Breck England, and Julie Schmidt.
    pages cm
  ISBN 978-1-941631-21-8 (paperback)
  1. Business presentations. 2. Business communication. 3. Communication in management. I. Title.
  HF5718.22.K647 2015
  658.4'52—dc23
                                                                    2015008819

Editing by Debbie Harmsen
Copyediting by James Fraleigh
Proofreading by Greg Teague and Jenny Bridges
Indexing by Jigsaw Indexing
Cover design by Sarah Dombrowsky and Bradford Foltz
Text design by Silver Feather Design
Text composition by PerfecType, Nashville, TN
Printed by Lake Book Manufacturing

Distributed by Perseus Distribution
www.perseusdistribution.com

To place orders through Perseus Distribution:
Tel: (800) 343-4499
Fax: (800) 351-5073
E-mail: orderentry@perseusbooks.com

Significant discounts for bulk sales are available. Please contact
Glenn Yeffeth at glenn@benbellabooks.com or (214) 750-3628.

CONTENTS

INTRODUCTION

Time: 2:30 in the afternoon on a Tuesday
Place: Conference room, headquarters of Fissile Co., an online retailer of ski equipment
Event: Staff meeting

Peter, a guy from finance, is giving a presentation to the dozen young executives who run the company. Let's tune into what he is saying and what his audience is thinking.

> **PETER** (finance guy): "I think this is a good time to go over some issues about credit card security . . . I have just a few slides . . ."

> **CLAIRE** (the CEO): *Credit cards. Hmm. I think mine is expiring next month. I suppose they'll send me a new one. Hope it doesn't get lost in the mail like the last time I moved. Really liked that apartment. Too bad I didn't hold on to it. Wonder how much I could've made by subletting it? Where's that calculator app? . . .*

> **PETER:** "Enhanced authorization includes data on internet protocol . . . and this is where our EBITDA is significantly impacted . . ."

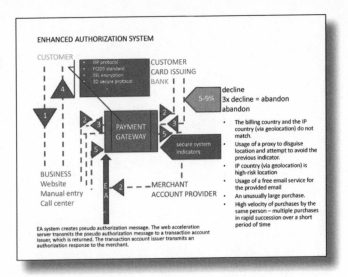

MAX (head of sales): *Enhanced. That's what Arliss wants. She wants an "enhanced" lifestyle. That means spending a load on plastic surgery, even though she's just fine the way she is, as I keep telling her . . .*

NEVA (company lawyer): [thumbing a text quietly under the table: *So the complaint went to court this morning. I'm about halfway through the pleading, respecting the motion for a preliminary injunction.*]

TAD (product director): *That is one ugly slide. I have absolutely no idea what all those numbers mean. I guess he'll explain them if they're important. Hey, he just said EBITDA. Claire used that word in the meeting yesterday . . . it's a number, that's all I know. I wonder what it means. No way am I going to ask . . .*

KIP (fulfillment manager): [Ring.] "Sorry, that's my phone. I've gotta take this." [He's out the door.]

PETER: "The additional data enriches our authorization decisions . . ."

AMITA (marketing person): *Isn't this meeting over yet? Here I am right in the middle of a campaign, the designers are making one mess after another, and with the holidays coming up . . .*

NEVILLE (IT manager): [Buzz. He looks at his phone.] *A text from Dexter. Probably another stupid video. He's too funny. The last one was him and his dog . . . Yeah, it's another video. What? He's followed his mother-in-law into a casino? This is going to be hilarious! I'll just mute this . . .*

ELLIE (the intern): *I've got to stay awake, I've got to stay awake, I've got to stay awake, I've got to stay awake, I'VE GOT TO STAY AWAKE . . . I wonder if it's possible to sleep with your eyes open . . .*

PETER: ". . . and when we prioritize our IT upgrade decisions, we ought to give top priority to enhanced authorization data."

QUENTIN (another finance guy): *. . . if we calculate the present value of the tax shield and the distress cost from the enterprise value we could come up with a purely operating multiple totally independent of our capital structure that would outweigh the cost of potential errors if left in place . . .*

PETER: ". . . So, this is why we have to address our credit card security."

CLAIRE: *Oh, I think he's finished. I wonder what that was all about.* "Well, okay. Thanks, Peter. Does anyone have any questions? No? Okay, then, I guess we can all get back to work now."

OUR SHRINKING ATTENTION SPANS

How many presentations like this have you sat through? Why are most presentations and the audience reactions to them just like what we read here?

In today's world of technology, the minute your audience is bored or confused, they can easily disappear into their smartphones or tablets to stay occupied. This means that when you're presenting, your audience is not at all captive. They are bombarded on all sides by people or things demanding to be noticed. They are constantly getting buzzed at, beeped at, blinked at, and distracted in every manner. It's become so commonplace that this is how the Urban Dictionary defines a presentation:

PRESENTATION /ˌprɛz ənˈteɪ ʃən, ˌpri zɛn-/: *A set number of agonizing minutes of exclusive divided attention (divided among you and your lousy slides, Facebook, Youtube [sic], email, Myspace [sic], text messages, chats, and other cool websites and iPhone apps) intended for explaining to a group of unwilling people what took you three weeks to partially understand and one night to put on PowerPoint.*

People's attention is now the scarcest commodity there is, which is ironic when half our time is spent communicating. As City University of New York (CUNY) professor Cathy Davidson points out, "We think we listen to what people are saying, but it turns out we're a little like dogs in that we sometimes hear the tone of voice and don't even pay attention to what that voice is actually saying."[1]

Our attention spans and emotional connections are under attack. The ease of communication has made the whole world part of our circle of contacts, but this convenience has its downside. Writer Jonathan Safran Foer told a group of college graduates, "Each step forward in technological communication has made things more convenient. But each step has also made it easier, just a little bit easier, to avoid the emotional work of being present. To write 'LOL' rather than to actually laugh out loud; to send a crying emoji rather than actually crying; to convey information rather than humanity. It's never been easier to say nothing."[2]

How do you get a message across and persuade people to action—real action—in a world like that?

We wrote this book to answer that question.

WE ARE ALL PRESENTERS

If you've ever been in a room like the one in Peter's speech scenario (and who hasn't?), you know that Peter was not *connecting* with his coworkers. Their minds and hearts were all elsewhere. Peter had a vitally important message to share, but virtually no one got it. It was just "one more meeting" with no good result.

And just like Peter, all of us are constantly making lousy presentations to each other, over and over. Yes, we are.

"Not me," you say. "I don't give that many presentations."

Lots of people say they don't present much, but they really do, more than they think.

Here's the actual definition of a presentation: *The sharing of information between two or more people with the intent to inform or persuade.*

We usually think of a presentation as a formal thing: You stand up in front of a room full of people, you speak, maybe you show slides, you answer questions, and then you sit down. It's something you "deliver." People do this many different ways, formally around a table or virtually around the globe.

But more often in today's world presentations are a lot less formal, like when you sit down for a quick status report, you're on the phone with a client, you're trying to make a point to your brother-in-law, or you're asking your boss for a raise. In all these cases, you have a message to convey. You are *sharing information with the intent to inform or persuade.* You are making a presentation.

In the Industrial Age, people worked with their hands. But today we live in an era of "knowledge work." We work with our brains, with words, and with pictures, and we spend at least half our time communicating with each other. This is how we create value in the Knowledge Age.

Ironically, as we all know, we're just not very good at it.

When we ask people why presentations fail, they always say the same things: lack of preparation, poor visuals, bad tools, overreliance on PowerPoint, reading the slides, disengaged delivery, lack of understanding of audience needs, no clear message. Sound familiar?

People just *expect* they're going to hear and see poor presentations.

What are poor presentations costing us? We're losing time: Think of all the prep time and audience time that's wasted—ever been to an "unproductive meeting" due to a poor presentation? And lost time means lost money. But even more important, *what great idea or innovation or sales opportunity never happens because people cannot communicate in a coherent and well-structured way?*

It stands to reason that people who *can* communicate will automatically have a competitive advantage.

THE PRESENTATION ADVANTAGE

The ability to give a persuasive presentation has been called "the top business skill" of our age. And "organizations that are highly effective at communication" are "more than twice as likely to significantly outperform their peers."[3] Obviously, there is such a thing as the presentation advantage.

How do you get your presentation to "stand out" in the middle of a constant stream of bad presentations? How do you create that sudden, sustained bond with people who would rather do almost anything than listen to another presentation? How do you gain the presentation advantage?

When you're presenting, you want a very specific outcome. You have a goal or purpose in mind, and, obviously, you've connected if you achieve your goal.

A story by Stephen R. Covey demonstrates this. He writes in his book, *The 7 Habits of Highly Effective People*, of an acquaintance of his who was frustrated about his boss' "unproductive leadership style":

"I've talked to him about it, he's aware of it, but he does nothing," he told me.

"Well, why don't you make an effective presentation?" I asked.

"I did," was the reply.

"How do you define 'effective'? Who do they send back to school when the salesman doesn't sell—the buyer? Effective means it works."[4]

An effective presentation starts with you. You are your message. If you know how to *connect*—you have passion around the content you've conveying, you are seen as someone with character and competence, and your audience is engaged with you no matter how tough the subject—then you've got what it takes to be a great communicator.

In this book we're going back to school for a while to figure out how to make an effective presentation—to learn what goes into a presentation that works, that creates a purposeful shift in knowledge or behavior. And in today's world, that could mean with just one other person or one hundred people, whether you're standing, sitting, or virtually present around the world.

We're going to look not only at how to connect with your message, your audience, and yourself, but also how to develop a powerful message, design impactful visuals, and deliver with excellence.

CHAPTER 1

THE FOUNDATION:
IT'S ALL ABOUT CONNECTING

WHEN YOU'RE PRESENTING, WHAT IS your ultimate objective? Would you believe that at the core, you have the same purpose no matter the topic of your presentation? It's true: The purpose of a presentation is to shift a paradigm.

Stephen R. Covey explained in *The 7 Habits of Highly Effective People* how the word "paradigm" originated from the Greek: "It was originally a scientific term, and is more commonly used today to mean a model, theory, perception, assumption, or frame of reference. In the more general sense, it's the way we 'see' the world—not in terms of our visual sense of sight, but in terms of perceiving, understanding, and interpreting."[5]

At FranklinCovey we talk a lot about paradigms and shifting them, and the reason we do is because getting someone to see things differently, to have a paradigm shift,

9

is essential for change to happen. Our paradigms control our behavior. If we have the paradigm that old movies are best, we'll avoid new ones. If we have the paradigm that executives speak double-talk, we won't believe what they tell us. If we have the paradigm that presentations on finance are boring, we'll sleep through them.

You can tell people wearing black lenses that the world isn't utterly dark, but simply telling them won't change their paradigm. They might even believe what you say, but their paradigm won't shift—and their behavior won't change—until somehow you get them to take off the black glasses and *see* things differently. Without a paradigm shift, they will go on walking slowly in circles and bumping into things.

In simple terms, your job as a presenter is to help people change the way they look at things, and thus their attitudes or behaviors. If you don't do that, your presentation isn't effective.

First, though, you need to shift your own paradigm around what it takes to create and deliver effective presentations. You must deeply believe that you must *connect* in three ways:

- Connect with your message
- Connect with yourself
- Connect with your audience

Most books on presentation skills will give you lots of tips on how to stand and deliver—how to control your voice, your posture, your mannerisms, and so forth. And

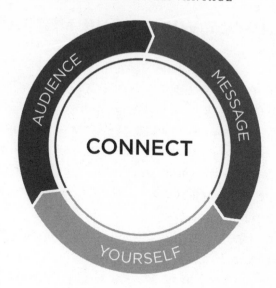

you'll get that here, too. But what you won't get from the other books is the real secret of making an effective presentation: *connecting with your message, with yourself, and with your audience.*

If you can do these things, you gain what we call the *presentation advantage.* You have not only the professional skills but also the trustworthy character of a presenter to whom people will really listen. It's one thing to be a slick presenter—it's another thing entirely to be a trusted advisor to people who count on you.

Our promise: If you make the mental connections we're talking about here *and* practice the skills in this book, you'll make effective presentations every time.

CONNECT WITH YOUR MESSAGE

What does it mean to "connect with your message?"

It means that you're driven by purpose and passion—that you care about what you're presenting.

What happens if you aren't connected to your message? You're bored, you're dull, and the audience feels no impact. Passion and motivation mean everything in a presentation. The more connected you are to your message, the higher the probability of success.

"But," you say, "I'm not passionate about this thing I have to present. I really can't get excited about this topic."

What you need to do is something poker players are familiar with: raise the ante.

Raise the Ante

The word "ante" means "before," and in poker, the ante is the money you have to throw into the pot up front just to get the right to play the game. By "raising the ante" in your presentation, we mean that you increase the stakes for the audience. Ask yourself, "What mission-critical strategic goal am I serving with this presentation?" You make it clear that your message *does* matter and you let your audience know what is at risk if they don't act.

Raising the ante is a powerful way to connect with your audience. It clearly shows them what is at stake if they do not act. This chart shows two possibilities: what happens when Peter, our finance guy, fails to connect, and what happens when he raises the ante. See the difference?

PETER	WHEN HE SAYS . . .	. . . HIS COWORKERS
Fails to connect	"I think this is a good time to go over some issues about credit card security . . . I have just a few slides. . . ."	Check out.
Raises the ante	"We're losing a million dollars a year."	Spill coffee, make choking noises, abruptly wake up, and listen!

You see, Peter knows that Fissile Co. is bleeding money because of credit card fraud, and he has a duty to make that reality as clear as possible to his coworkers. He needs to raise the ante.

The same is true for you. If you always give a presentation that is strategically important, people will listen to you. You'll be the one running up the highway to tell oncoming traffic that the bridge is out. In other words, you'll be the one who's always *worth* listening to, and you'll have the presentation advantage.

What we're saying is, connect to audiences with the *real* message. Ask yourself what's at stake if the paradigm doesn't shift and people go on without hearing you. What will happen to them? What will happen to your organization?

If you start a strategic presentation as if it's a tactical issue, you're doing your audience no favor. You don't start with, "Hey, would this be a good time to talk about road conditions ahead?" if you're trying to tell people that the bridge is out.

"But I don't give strategic presentations," you say. Or maybe you're thinking, "Strategy? That's way above my pay grade."

Every organization has—or should have—dreams, strategies, and goals, and your job is to help make those happen. Always frame your presentation in terms of those strategic issues; never downplay the power of your *real* message. Why didn't Peter connect in the first place? Because he mistook a strategic issue for a tactical one. His message was not really about "enhancing authorization data" (whatever that is); it was about keeping thieves from stealing millions from the company's bottom line. But that message never got through. It didn't *connect*.

Never give a presentation that isn't strategic. For example, if you're asking for a raise, you're not simply asking for more money; you're describing the value you bring to the company and how you will continue to contribute. If your message is merely tactical, find some other way than getting up on a stage to pass the information to people who can use it.

But if the game is important, if the stakes are strategic, if your message really does matter, let your energy show. You are deeply invested in it. You have vital information that decision makers need. You have a meaningful presentation to give that will have a positive impact on others. Tell it like it is. Say what's really at stake. Give it to your listeners so clearly that they would have to be doorknobs to miss it.

>>> *To connect with your message:*

- Raise the ante. Connect your message to things that matter: the organization's mission and goals. Get to the point. Tell people the truth they need to hear.

- Distinguish a tactical message from a strategic message. *Don't* give tactical presentations—find some other way to pass on the information. *Do* give strategic presentations—it's your job.

CONNECT WITH YOURSELF

What does it mean to "connect with yourself"?

It means that you are at one with yourself. You tell the truth. You don't have a hidden agenda or "two faces." You know what you're talking about, or you admit it if you don't. We can trust what you say.

Your credibility depends on two things: your character and your competence. In the words of Stephen M. R. Covey, "Character includes your integrity, your motive, your intent with people. Competence includes your capabilities, your skills, your track record. And both are vital . . . You might think a person is sincere, even honest, but you won't trust that person fully if he or she doesn't get results. And the opposite is true. A person might have great skills and talents, but if he or she is not honest, you're not going to trust that person either."[6]

To connect with yourself, you must have a trustworthy character. You must also be competent—in your subject and in your presentation skills.

What happens if you aren't connected with yourself?

You come across as untrustworthy, unbelievable, possibly incompetent—and as a person who may not have the best intentions. You become "incredible," which is *not* a compliment.

But your effect on others is really only a secondary issue.

To be connected with yourself means you are credible *to* yourself. Your credibility comes from the inside out. You trust yourself to tell the truth, to talk straight, to be transparent about your agenda, to know your subject, and serve your audience as if they were your best customers. You show "one face," and it's a real face.

Staying out of the "Spin Cycle"

Lots of communication experts will argue that this view is naïve—that we live in a "post-truth" age of political and commercial "spin," so we have to play the game. Some of these experts argue that a sophisticated presenter knows just how to spin the message and that truth is a meaningless concept anyway. It used to be said that you were entitled to your own opinion but not your own facts; today, too many people make up their own facts.

Obviously, it's hard to see the whole truth of anything. As we said earlier, what we see depends on our paradigms. Wearing dark glasses makes the world *look* dark, but that doesn't mean the world *is* dark. There is still an objective truth, and presenters with character do their best to help people see it. They don't persuade people to swap one pair of colored glasses for another—they persuade them to take off the glasses and see the world as it is.

Here's how people (including perhaps you?) spin the message:

> "The great enemy of clear language is insincerity."
> —GEORGE ORWELL

- **Cherry-picking:** Select only favorable evidence to prop up your side and unfavorable evidence to pull down the other side. Here's an example:

CUSTOMER	SELLER
Why should I buy this new program?	Because it integrates well with what you already have, and it is showing great results.

What the seller did not say was that it is not yet tested and they have had some suspicious issues with a few customers that may or may not have long-range ramifications.

- **Doublespeak:** Using words that mean the opposite of what is intended. When you say one thing, but really mean something else, that's doublespeak.

WHEN YOU SAY . . .	WHAT YOU REALLY MEAN IS . . .
"It's coming along."	"I haven't started yet."
"Interesting idea."	"Useless idea."
"That's a great question."	"That's a dumb question."
"She's an independent voice."	"She's a troublemaker."
"I'll take that under advisement."	"Forget that."
"I'm glad you asked me that."	"I was hoping nobody would ask me that."

- **Euphemisms:** Making bad news sound like good news, or at least not so bad.

EUPHEMISM	WHAT IT REALLY MEANS
"We're going to give our customers a more independent buying experience."	"We're laying people off."
"Our customers are still evaluating the benefits of our premium products."	"We've priced ourselves out of the market."
"We're going to eliminate some of the distortions in our tax code."	"We're going to raise taxes."

EUPHEMISM	WHAT IT REALLY MEANS
"Market conditions have not yet aligned to our projections."	"Nobody's buying our stuff."
"Our previous statements on this subject are no longer operative."	"We told a bunch of lies."
"He's pursuing other opportunities."	"He's been terminated."

Once you start spinning, you're in danger of falling into a "spin cycle," where you need more and more spin to survive. People and organizations that try to color or cover up the truth inevitably have to keep up the façade until the truth catches up with them. There is no good way to spin the truth.

Besides, the whole idea of spin is backfiring on the people who do it. The age of spin has turned us into skeptics; according to a global survey, "less than one fifth of the general public believes business leaders and government officials will tell the truth."[7] Malcolm Gladwell points out that "[W]e seldom consider whether spin works. We simply assume that, because people are everywhere trying to manipulate us, we're being manipulated." He believes that the more spin people are subjected to, the less likely they are to fall for it: "The louder and faster the whirring of the spinners becomes, the more effective clarity and plain-spokenness will be."[8]

So how do you keep yourself from falling into the spin cycle?

You stay true to yourself by staying true to principles. In the world we live in, you will have the presentation advantage if you are honest and plain spoken.

The temptation to spin things is strong. If you feel misunderstood, you might be tempted to overcorrect with a little spin. Instead, figure out how to tell your story better. If you feel out of your depth on some issue, don't pull "facts" out of the air. Instead, admit you're not ready to answer and go find out what you need to know. If you feel that telling the truth would be disloyal to some people, be assured that your loyalty to the truth is a higher principle. If you have bad news, don't hide it under a pile of euphemisms. Come out with it. People are usually more forgiving than you expect, but even if they aren't, you still have your integrity—and that's worth more than anything.

> "I know how easy it is for one to stay well within moral, ethical, and legal bounds through the skillful use of words—and to thereby spin, sidestep, circumvent, or bend a truth completely out of shape."
> —SIDNEY POITIER

If you look through the dozens of books on the market about presentation skills, you will find that none of them even mentions the character issues we've talked about here. Do a word search on them. Nowhere do they talk about things like integrity, honesty, or trust. You'll get lots of good ideas on how to organize and deliver your presentation (as you will here), but nothing whatsoever about what matters most to your audience: Can you be trusted?

You can be the slickest of presenters, but if you're not trustworthy, you will shift no paradigms.

Doing Your "Real Job"

If you're going to ask people to shift their paradigm, you need to make sure your paradigm is better. That's a question of your competence—do you really know whereof you speak? How sure of your facts are you? Are you adequately prepared to give a presentation? Have you paid the price in terms of research, experience, and practice?

"Winging it" is not a good idea. Think of your audience as your customers: they need the best service you can give. You wouldn't want your doctor or your hairdresser or your airline pilot to be just winging it, and you shouldn't either if you're going to serve people well. As Mark Twain said, "I never could make a good impromptu speech without several hours to prepare it."

How do you know your paradigm is better?

Again, your paradigm is effective if it aligns with principles. In other words, it makes better sense in the real world than the paradigm your listeners hold.

Peter the finance guy has actually done good work in getting ready for his presentation. He has a firm fix on reality. He has double-checked his data to make sure he's right. He knows why the company is losing a million dollars a year, and he knows how to stop the bleeding. But to do that, he's got to persuade the executive team to change a paradigm.

That's the part of his job he *didn't* do.

In other words, Peter is clearly good at his job, but only if you define his job as analyzing numbers. Peter was not hired to do math problems—he was hired to tell stories.

That's right. He was hired to communicate to others the story that the numbers tell him.

A major manufacturing firm once asked to meet with one of our consultants, an expert in presentation skills. The senior vice president said, "We hire about three hundred new engineers every year right out of college, and I'd like to introduce you to some of them."

The next thing our consultant knew, he was being marched into a room full of young men and women who looked up eagerly as he and the vice president entered.

The vice president took the podium. "Good morning, everyone. Congratulations—this is your first day on the job. Every one of you was hired because you're the cream of the crop. You're all bright, and some of you are even math geniuses. You bring terrific, fresh new ideas. I imagine many of you think you were hired to do exotic programming and invent amazing things.

"Actually, that's only half your job. The other half is to communicate your fresh new solutions to the rest of us. You have to be able to stand and deliver, to talk intelligently and persuasively, and to convince people of the value of your ideas.

"This man here," he said, pointing to our consultant, "is going to explain your job to you. You'll be working with him for the next few weeks, and if he says we should keep you, we will. If not . . . well, good luck everyone." And the vice president left the room.

* * *

In the age of knowledge work, knowledge is the source of value. But knowledge is no good to the world if it isn't shared effectively. That's the real job to be done. It's crucial to have good technical skills—you need them—and if you add the character of a trustworthy person, you'll have the *presentation advantage*.

If not . . . well, good luck.

››› *To connect with yourself:*

- Develop both the character and the competence of a trustworthy person.
- Stay out of the "spin cycle"—be plain spoken and honest.
- Learn the "real job" of a knowledge worker—how to tell a story with excellence.

CONNECT WITH YOUR AUDIENCE

What does it mean to "connect with your audience"?

It means that you get their attention and keep it. This is easier said than done. According to those who know, this is what's happening to adult attention spans[9]:

Average attention span in 2000	12 seconds
Average attention span in 2013	8 seconds

If the adult attention span is dropping that fast and people are checking their phones every two minutes, you're going to have a problem connecting to your average listeners.

So you've got maybe eight seconds to grab your audience before they float away on a river of distractions. Then you need to tighten the connection or you'll lose them, with the resulting loss of time, effort, credibility, and your good ideas.

And you need to make that connection standing up, sitting down, in the hallway, over lunch, or online.

Once you have the attention of your audience, they become your allies and advocates. They shift their paradigms. Then they actually do what you've asked them to do.

You can be very connected with your message. You can have character and competence. But unless you connect with your audience, you're not effective yet.

Why did Peter the finance guy fail to connect with his audience?

For a couple of reasons. First, he didn't have the skill to engage them. Although he knew his stuff, he seemed disconnected from his own message—no passion, no energy. He talked over their heads, using lots of business and accounting gobbledygook. He didn't know how to tell others the story that his numbers were telling him, so he lost them from the beginning.

As you work through this book, you'll discover how to engage and *reengage* your audience. You do that by turning your presentation into a *conversation*. Don't lecture people, talk with them. Go around the room and connect with people—with their eyes, their minds, their hearts. If you feel like you're losing that connection, reconnect.

Peter's second problem is that he's talking to a twenty-first-century audience:

- People check their cell phones on average 110 times during the daylight hours.[10]

- Around 100 billion business emails are sent every day—and growing.[11]

- Businesspeople between 25 and 34 send or receive 2,240 texts per month—double that for people under 25.[12]

Peter has trouble connecting because his listeners are constantly connected with something else. We've talked about our microscopic attention span. It's so ironic in a world where we're connected 24/7 that we have trouble connecting with the people sitting right in front of us. But nobody in history has been as distracted as we are.

It just gets worse if you have to deliver *virtually*; that is, online or in a telephone conference.

If you're presenting online to ten people in a virtual meeting, two of them are probably checking their email, another one is surfing the web, one is playing a game, and six of them are checking in and out mentally. You can't look into anyone's eyes. You can't watch their nonverbal behavior. You can't sense if they're paying attention or not. It's really hard to connect without contact—a remote audience is already physically disconnected from you, and if the presentation is deadly boring, the mental and emotional connection breaks down, too.

Of course, Peter can't control the multiply distracted environment we all live in. But it doesn't help that he's up there focusing on himself—and meanwhile, there goes the audience.

There are things you can do to keep people engaged. This book will help you overcome the distractions when you're presenting, and maybe even make all of the technology in the room work for you instead of against you.

So how do we engage and reengage the audience no matter what the distractions?

Well, let's see what happens when Peter has another chance to talk to his coworkers. It's a few days after his first presentation, and he knows he didn't connect the first time, so this time at the staff meeting, he's ready to take a different approach:

> **PETER** (finance guy): "Who can tell me what this slide means?"

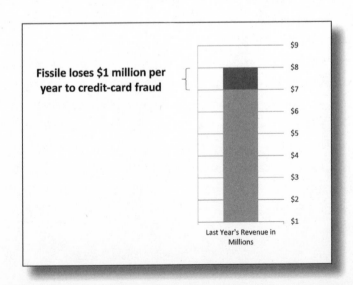

AMITA (the marketing person): *Ohmygosh, we lost a million dollars this year!*

CLAIRE (the CEO): "It means we lost a million dollars this year from credit card fraud."

PETER: "Exactly. I've got two points today. First, I want to show you why we're losing that kind of money, and second, how we can stop the bleeding. How many of you feel like this is a problem we should solve?"

ALL: [Hands go up, except for . . .]

QUENTIN (the other finance guy): "Oh come on, Peter, everybody gets hit with credit card fraud. We've got the same security everybody else has. All you can do is live with it."

PETER: "You're right. Fraudsters do hit everybody, but what do you think about the next slide? What does this mean?"

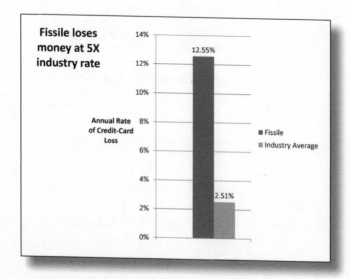

MAX (the head of sales): *What the . . . We're five times worse than the industry average!*

NEVA (the company lawyer): "We're losing five times more than most other online retailers."

TAD (the product director): *Now these are numbers I can understand . . .*

KIP (the fulfillment manager): "Why are we so much worse, Peter?" [Ring.] "Oh, sorry, that's my phone. I'll turn it off."

PETER: "Our security system is too weak. Let me show you why . . .

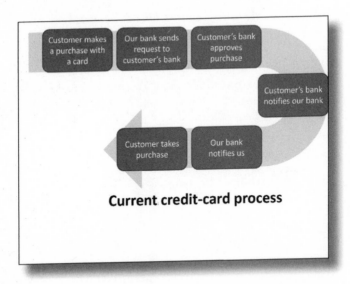

Current credit-card process

"Can you see what happens when a cardholder makes a purchase from us? The purchaser enters this information, our system checks it against the purchaser's billing and shipping address, and we accept or decline it.

"The problem is, thieves can easily steal your card number and address. To sum up, our card security is very low. Now here's the solution.

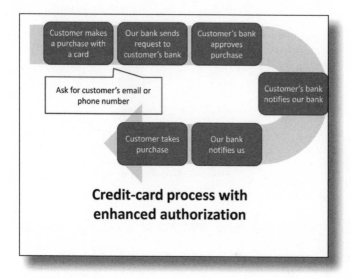

Credit-card process with enhanced authorization

"Other retailers are doing 'enhanced authorization.' It simply means getting more data from the customer that's harder to steal, like the customer's email address, a phone number, the name of their internet provider, the name of their favorite pet— that sort of thing."

NEVILLE (the IT manager): [Ring.] *Dexter again? Who cares about his dog, let me shut this off.* "You mean customers would have to enter all that info every time they make a purchase?"

PETER: "No, they wouldn't. They'd enter it one time in a profile and then we'd ask a random security question when they make a purchase."

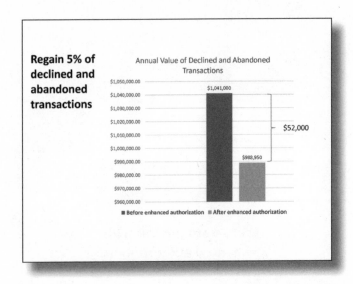

"Not only would it save money, it might make more money. We'd actually approve more purchases. Right now, we decline a lot of credit cards because we're suspicious. With enhanced authorization, we don't need to be so suspicious, and I estimate we'll approve at least 5 percent more transactions. So it makes sense to get enhanced authorization in place right away."

ELLIE (the intern): *That does make sense. I wonder if my credit card is safe. Golly, the things you learn in a business meeting!*

With Enhanced Authorization:

- Stop losing $1 million/year to credit-card fraud
- Cut our loss rate from one of the worst to one of the best in industry
- Add $52,000 revenue lost because of declined/abandoned transactions (estimated)

PETER: "It will take some efforts from the web developers to change our system. But if we get enhanced authorization in place, we should be able to increase revenue *and* save a million dollars next year. I recommend we act now before we lose more money. Any questions?"

NEVILLE: "Yes. Our IT department is already backed up with projects. Do you think this should change our priorities?"

CLAIRE: "I think it definitely takes priority. What do you all think? Everyone agrees? Well, okay— Neville, why don't you get with Peter and bring us a project plan right away?"

Do you think Peter connected with his audience this time? What did he do differently? How do you know he was effective this time? Why? Did he succeed in shifting a paradigm?

What Peter did was not rocket science. He didn't have to turn into a slick, suave speaker, and he didn't have to fill his presentation with sophisticated special effects to entertain people. But he did have to connect with his message, himself, and his audience.

HOW TO MAKE THE CONNECTIONS: THE 3 "D"S

This book contains a three-phase process that will help you make those connections. In fact, the book is organized around those three phases:

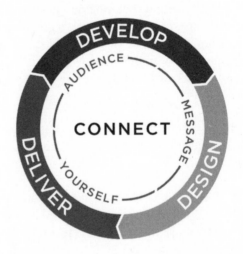

- Develop a powerful message
- Design impactful visuals
- Deliver with excellence

Each phase of the process contains steps and tools that will help you connect, whether it is one person or one hundred, be they standing or sitting in front of you, or online around the world.

CHAPTER 2

DEVELOP A POWERFUL MESSAGE

THE MOMENT THE PLANE TOUCHED down in Las Vegas, the passengers were up and grabbing their luggage. It was the weekend special, and people were itching to get off the plane and out to the shows and the casinos. Then they heard the firm voice of a flight attendant over the intercom:

"Ladies and gentlemen, look out the window!"

The passengers stretched their necks to look outside.

"Do you see how fast we're going?"

They all nodded in unison. The plane was still rocketing down the runway.

"When the pilot puts on the brakes, you're all going to fly down this aisle and smash your skulls on the bulkhead. Now get back in your seats and put your belts on!"

They did.

This is what we call an effective presentation. This flight attendant could have dealt with the situation differently. She could have sweetly reminded them (in standard fashion) to "remain seated with your seatbelts securely fastened" and been ignored. She could have thrown up her hands and disregarded the dangers. Instead, she chose to get the results she wanted.

That's what a powerful message does. So many messages we hear lack power. If you fly on airplanes, you know that flight attendants give the same required security speech at the beginning of each flight, and nearly everybody tunes it out while they play with their phones or do the crossword in the airline magazine. To their credit, some airlines add humor so people will pay more attention, but the message has become so "formula" that it loses its power.

> "Those who tell the stories rule the world."
> —NATIVE AMERICAN PROVERB

By contrast, our Las Vegas flight attendant was a master of the "powerful message"—and developing a powerful message is the first requirement if you're going to connect with your audience.

Of course, the presentations you give are probably a lot more involved than hers, but the same principle she applied will work for you, too.

The principle the flight attendant followed is "Tell a Good Story."

TELL A GOOD STORY, NOT ODTAA

Most presentations are not *stories*, so nobody pays attention. When you were a kid, all adults sounded like the babbling parents on the *Peanuts* TV shows (and they still do, as we all know). But as soon as your mom or dad or Uncle Willy started telling a story, you were hypnotized. Do you think that changed when you grew up?

It didn't.

Consider this: The standard airplane safety demonstration consists more or less of seventeen items: ten instructions and seven reminders, all disconnected from each other. Like pieces of driftwood on a river, they pass randomly by most listeners. The presentation creates no pictures in the mind's eye. It tells no story. And most people ignore it.

> "Stories are data with a soul."
> —DR. BRENÉ BROWN, professor, speaker, and author

Years ago, the English novelist John Masefield wrote a whole book without a plot, filling it instead with random, disconnected "happenings." He called it *ODTAA*—short for "One Damn Thing after Another." Of course, Masefield did this as a joke, but how many presentations have you sat through that were just ODTAA?

It's the way most people present—random lists of bullet points. No story.

In her safety speech, our flight attendant, instead of mouthing a random set of reminders—ODTAA—she told a story. She grabbed passengers' attention and told them in graphic detail what was about to happen. And it worked.

But, you say, "Her story was really short. My presentation is long."

Think about it. In this era of sidetracked brains, which is going to work best for you: a short, impactful story with a tight structure, or a flood of bullet points passing like ODTAA before the glazed-over gaze of your audience?

"But I have a lot of stuff to cover," you say.

Fine. But tell the story first; then your listeners will *want* to hear the rest.

Our flight attendant didn't have time to explain the reasoning behind her request—to go over the laws of motion and inertia and arrive at a logical conclusion. That sort of presentation might be fine in a different setting, such as a meeting of scientists. So you have to ask yourself, what sort of story should you tell? Most of the time, easily distracted businesspeople need you to get to the point *now* and save the background stuff for later.

> **"Stories are the most powerful way to put ideas into the world."**
> —ROBERT MCKEE

Pull the Rug Out

Stories are usually simple. In the words of writing teacher Robert McKee, "A story begins when something throws life out of balance, and everything to restore the balance discovers the truth of life."[13]

Have you ever lost your balance? You trip on a crack in the sidewalk or somebody pulls the rug out from under you—and instantly your entire body panics. Your arms fly out, you dance like crazy, and you probably scream, too.

Until you get it back, your balance is all you care about. Well, your job as a presenter is to throw everyone off balance so they will care about your message.

In his first presentation, Peter the finance guy didn't throw everyone off balance, so they just didn't care. But in his second presentation, Peter wasted no time in showing everybody how the company was off balance—they were losing a million dollars a year, and to restore the balance, they would have to take steps to combat fraud. That's it. That's the story. But it was compelling enough to motivate action, which was the whole point.

So what's your story? What's your equivalent of "pulling the rug out" from under your listeners?

> "Words presented in a logically organized, hierarchical structure are much better remembered than words placed randomly—typically 40 percent better."
> —JOHN MEDINA

Two Things about the Brain

Always remember two things about the brains of your listeners.

First, they're not paying attention. It's not that they don't want to (well, maybe some don't), it's that they live in a hyper-distracted world and their attention spans are tiny. Although the brain is a miraculous sponge of information, it lets only a little bit in at a time.

Second, it's even worse than that. The part of the brain that lets in information allows only one thing in at a time, so if an audience member is looking at her phone, she's simply not listening to you. Don't be fooled when they say they're "multitasking." Brain scientists tell us that "multitasking, when it comes to paying attention, is a myth. The brain naturally focuses on concepts sequentially, one at a time."[14]

Because of the way the brain works, you need to throw the audience off balance immediately and *keep* them off balance or you'll lose them. Experts will tell you to "engage and reengage" the audience continually. To do that, you can construct your message carefully with logical organization and emotional power—or you can go home. This is a price you have to pay.

To develop a powerful message, you need these five skills. They're simple and logical, and every effective presenter has them.

5 Skills for Developing a Powerful Message

1. Define the purpose of your message.
2. Analyze your audience.
3. Consider logistics.
4. Develop strong key points.
5. Create a memorable introduction and conclusion.

DEFINE THE PURPOSE OF YOUR MESSAGE

So what made the Las Vegas flight attendant's message so powerful? How did she get immediate action from her audience?

She told them exactly what she wanted them to *do*. And she told them what they needed to *know* that would make them *feel* like doing that.

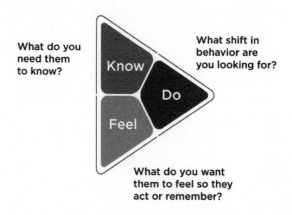

What do you need them to know?

What shift in behavior are you looking for?

What do you want them to feel so they act or remember?

To get people to *do* something, you need to figure out what they need to *know* that will make them *feel* like doing that thing. In the language of the experts, you "alter their paradigm so that their behavior changes." Knowledge alone doesn't necessarily shift a paradigm—think of all the people who know very well that overeating is bad for their health but go back to the buffet line anyway. Emotion alone doesn't always do the job, either—think of all the New Year's resolutions you've made in the "emotion of the moment" and then forgot about when the emotion passed.

"Begin with the end in mind."
—STEPHEN R. COVEY

But knowledge and emotion together—that's a recipe for changing people's paradigms, which in turn leads them to do things differently.

Think about it. You've been doing this intuitively all your life. Remember when you were a teenager trying to persuade your parents to let you do something you wanted to do? You let them *know* enough information so they would *feel* safe enough to let you *do* what you wanted—stay out late, go dancing, whatever. And if you were smart, it worked.

Let's see how our flight attendant used this formula: She gave them information ("Look out the window . . . do you see how fast we're going?"). She made the information emotionally powerful to *them* ("You're all going to fly down the aisle and smash your skulls."). And she made the call to action perfectly clear ("Get back in your seats and put your belts on!"). Do, know, feel. Simple.

She made people care enough to act. That's what you need to do.

So what end do you have in mind? What results do you want? What do you want people to do after listening to your presentation? What are you going to tell them that will make them feel like doing that?

What story can you tell that will move your audience to action?

The Bottom Line, Up Front

The story you tell must start with the bottom line.

Busy people want to know what's what, and they want to know now. Advertisers who spend millions studying the "science of attention" believe they have at most 6.5 seconds to "capture the consumer's attention and motivate them to act."[15] That's why it's usually best to start with your main point:

"We're losing a million dollars a year."

"You're all going to fly down the aisle and smash your skulls on the bulkhead."

Then give your reasons for your bottom-line message. Most of your listeners will appreciate it—or they won't be listeners for long.

As the savvy young director of marketing for Fissile, Amita was obsessed with finding new advantages in the market for her line of skiwear. Even with so many competitors jostling for space on retail shelves, she was confident and excited.

Her friends in the business weren't so confident. "How are you going to compete? It's a saturated market. There are so many big players and you're relatively new and regional. How can you hope to break out with your brand?"

Amita had learned how to look sure and self-possessed even when she didn't know what to do next—that was part of her success. However, most of her success was due to proactive thinking: "I know it's a tough market. But our customers' lives aren't perfect, are they?" In other words, she knew that her customers had a lot of struggles. What could she do help them win?

She paid the price to learn. After a lot of work, she found that the little-known Fissile brand was respected but mostly overlooked. Fissile products were considered high quality—nothing wrong with them—there was just no particular market advantage in carrying them. As a result, Fissile skiwear hung on the low hangers and sat on the back

> develop

shelves of the giant recreational outlets and department stores.

So for Amita, this was the question: What bottom-line battle were her customers fighting? How could she get her products front and center in that battle?

> "When you deliver information the way the other person wants to receive it, you increase your bottom line."
> —LISA A. MININNI

Oddly enough, she found the answer not out on the shelves but in the backroom.

Everyone knows that retail stores fight the inventory battle constantly: "How much product should we order? How much is enough? How much is too much? Suppose we run out? Suppose we end up with more than we can sell? All that stuff on the shelves is cash sitting there and losing value—it's got to move." The ideal is to move product out the door as fast as it comes in, but until someone invents a crystal ball, it's hard to tell how much product you'll need.

So Amita prepared a presentation to show how she could help her customers win the "Battle of Inventory." It went like this:

> **AMITA:** "I'm not really here to talk about my products. Not today. You're fighting the inventory battle, and I'd like to show you how Fissile can help you win that battle in a big way.
>
> "Research shows that having too much inventory on your shelves costs you about a third of its value every year. On the other hand, having too little inventory hurts you, too. For every hour you're out of stock, you lose sales. You know how much out-of-stocks are costing you.

"At Fissile, we've made a science out of making sure you always have exactly the right amount of product that you'll need at any moment—no more, no less."

Amita went on to tell the story of how her company could keep that promise, but her buyers were already sold. She got tons of new orders. What made the difference? The obvious fact that she was there to help them win their biggest battle rather than to push more of her product and make the problem worse.

She showed the buyers how they could be heroes—how they, with her help, could make a solid contribution to their *own* bottom line. It was a big win-win.

So where is the bottom line for your listeners? What paradigm are you trying to shift and replace with a better paradigm? How can you make your listeners into the heroes of their own story?

The Bottom Line Ignored

Now here's Tad, the product director at Fissile Co., giving a presentation to some people in the market for racing suits for competitive skiers. Tad is as bright as they come in the world of engineering sports equipment. He knows how smart he is. An expert athlete himself, he's made a science out of high performance on the ski slopes—he uses exotic tools like electron microscopes and magnetic-resonance imaging to design "aerodynamic fabrics." A high-energy, impatient sort of person, he talks to himself a lot and isn't a very good listener.

Anyway, Tad feels like he's made a real breakthrough with a new suit he calls "The Missile" and the customers have given him ten minutes to show it off:

> **TAD:** "Thanks for the opportunity to go over some of the features of our new product. I have just a few slides. From this slide you can see that the primary new feature of my Fissile Missile suit is enhanced permeability.
>
> "The zippers and seams are placed to raise the permeability factor by about two liters per meter squared per second. Additionally, the suit is slightly undersized because force measurements are sensitive to suit size and make a difference of about 7 percent in aerodynamic drag, as this slide indicates. By undersizing we can enhance permeability by at least two liters and maybe more.
>
> "But the real breakthrough is a textured, dimpled-knit sharkskin structure. Under an electronic microscope in the wind tunnel this structure appears to enable about seven liters of additional permeability over a 250-meter glide course.
>
> "Thanks again, and I'll take any questions you have now."

By this point, they had no questions. They were all playing with their phones.

What do you think? How did he use his ten minutes? Has he sold his listeners? Has he made it easier or harder for them to make a decision? What story has he told them? What end did he have in mind? Has he achieved his purpose?

The first thing we need to do is get clear on who our audience is and what the point of our presentation is: Is it to shift their knowledge or, as it is in most cases, shift their behavior?

Then we are prepared to ask ourselves the purpose questions: Do, Know, Feel.

Of course, Tad's end in mind—his "Do"—should be obvious with this audience. He wants these people to buy his suits. But what does he give them in terms of a "Know" and a "Feel"? How intensely do they feel about buying his suits?

Meh. Not very.

And what do they know now that they didn't know before? That Tad's suits are more snug and permeable than they used to be—although they'd have to do a lot of mental math to figure out just how much more.

So what? Obviously, permeability is very important to Tad and he knows all about it, but why should his listeners care about it? His "end in mind" is not theirs. It's simply not their battle.

> "The greatest story commandment: Make me care."
> —ANDREW STANTON, filmmaker

The So-What Factor

In every presentation, all the listeners wear an invisible sign on their foreheads. There are two words on this sign:

So what?

That's everybody's question as you stand up in front of them. They are pleading with you to tell them "so what?"—to get to the bottom line—to give them something to care about, to motivate them, to inspire them with a new paradigm.

When Peter the finance guy gave his second presentation, he made the audience care. The "so what?" was that they were losing a million dollars a year, five times more than their competitors were losing. That's a big "so what?"

Of course, the "so what?" is always relative. In a vast multinational corporation, a million-dollar loss is far less significant than it is to a smaller company like Fissile Co. So you have to ask yourself, "What do *these people in front of me* need to know that will make them feel like doing something?"

> "Most people don't listen with the intent to understand; they listen with the intent to reply."
> —STEPHEN R. COVEY

The underlying principle here is *motivation*—people won't act if they don't feel emotionally driven to act. They have to feel excited or dangerously out of balance. As Stephen R. Covey taught, "This is one of the greatest insights in the field of human motivation: Satisfied needs do not motivate. It's only the unsatisfied need that motivates."[16]

Use our Presentation Planner to decide how to motivate your audience to achieve your purpose. See how Peter used it on the next page. (You'll find a blank Presentation Planner at the end of this chapter.)

So, what should Tad have told his audience? What information would have made them feel like buying his suits?

In order to know that, he has to do a solid job of analyzing his audience.

TOPIC: DATE OF PRESENTATION:

DEFINE YOUR PURPOSE

WHO IS YOUR AUDIENCE?

THE INTENT OF YOUR PRESENTATION IS TO:

Persuade ☐ Inform ☐

WHAT DO YOU WANT YOUR AUDIENCE TO ...

Do? To authorize enhanced security measures against fraud.

Know? We're losing $1 million/year, which is 4-5 times more than others are losing. Also, we could make more revenue by accepting more credit card orders.

Feel? Urgency!!!

THE PURPOSE OF YOUR PRESENTATION IS:

ANALYZE YOUR AUDIENCE

One of the great experts on communication was Henry M. Boettinger. Years ago he attended a conference where lots of different people gave presentations. Here is what he said about it: "All were persons of intelligence, having something worthwhile to say, but the range of persuasive skill ran from embarrassing, painful failures (including cases of physical collapse) to skillful performers whose presentations were perfectly tuned to their audiences, and who made changing your mind an exhilarating experience.

"What makes the difference? Neither schooling, material, nor rank—of this I'm sure. Whether the audience was one or a thousand, success invariably attended only those who both understood and presented their ideas from the viewpoint of the needs and characteristics of the persons in their audience."[17]

So it didn't matter how educated they were. It didn't matter what they talked about. It didn't matter what their position was. What mattered was whether or not they were "tuned to the audience." Those were the presenters who made "changing your mind an exhilarating experience."

Tad wasn't tuned to the audience when he gave his presentation on ski-racing suits. We know that because they were not exhilarated—they were deeply buried in their smartphones.

So how do you get tuned to the audience? How do you present your ideas from the viewpoints of the audience members? You're not a mind reader. How can you find out their priorities?

Seek First to Understand

Learn to empathize with your audience. This is perhaps the most important thing you can do to become an effective presenter.

You have empathy when you truly *understand* people—not only what they think and say but what they feel.

This story from Stephen R. Covey illustrates the importance of the principle of empathy when you're making a presentation:

An acquaintance, a university professor, approached me one day and said, "Stephen, I can't get to first base in getting the funding I need for my research because my research is really not in the mainstream of this department's interests." After discussing his situation at some length, I suggested that he develop an effective presentation . . . "I know you're sincere and the research you want to do would bring great benefits. Describe the alternative they are in favor of better than they can themselves. Show that you understand them in depth. Then carefully explain the logic behind your request."

"Well, I'll try," he said.

"Do you want to practice with me?" I asked. He was willing, and so we dress rehearsed his approach.

When he went in to make his presentation, he started by saying, "Now let me see if I first understand what your objectives are, and what your concerns are about this presentation and my recommendation."

He took the time to do it slowly, gradually. In the middle of his presentation, demonstrating his depth of understanding and respect for their point of view, a senior professor turned to another professor, nodded, turned back to him and said, "You've got your money."[18]

By showing empathy for the decision makers, by meeting them mentally and emotionally where they were, the professor created a win for himself and them. By connecting to the priorities of your audience, you're more likely to achieve your own priorities.

Not everyone has the time to do this kind of preparation. Maybe you just found out you have to present tomorrow.

Or you've got thirty minutes to get ready. Or there are fifty people in the room and they all have different priorities.

Your presentation will succeed only if you can connect to those priorities—no connection, no success, even if you have just a few minutes to prepare.

Your Presentation Planner can help you analyze your audience in a matter of minutes:

ANALYZE YOUR AUDIENCE

WHAT DO THEY KNOW?
About the topic?

About you?

WHAT IS THEIR BIAS?
Toward the subject?

WHAT ARE THEIR PRIORITIES?

WHAT'S YOUR PURPOSE?

PURPOSE STATEMENT:

How do you get answers to the questions that provide the key insight to get us to the purpose statement?

Guess, if you have to. Suppose you've just been asked to speak to some clients who showed up without notice. Grab this form and think through each question. You'll be surprised—this little exercise will get your thoughts in order and you'll be ready.

If you have more time to prepare, phone some or all of your audience members and talk to them about their priorities. Google them. Find out who they are and get as granular as you can. What's on Twitter? Get into social media and learn about these people so you can tailor the experience for them and serve them better.

By analyzing your audience, you find out their level of knowledge, their biases, and their priorities. By connecting these things to your own purpose, you can create a "win-win" presentation—in other words, both you and your audience will get the results you all want. People with a win-win paradigm are the best presenters because they don't see their own win as separate from a win for the audience.

Let's look at this planner a little more closely.

The Expert Syndrome

Why ask what they already know about the topic? To avoid wasting their time on things they don't need to hear. Some presenters make the mistake of covering ground the audience already knows well.

On the other hand, don't overestimate the knowledge of your audience, particularly in your choice of language. Avoid using terminology the audience might not know. Remember Peter's first presentation, so full of jargon that people in the room couldn't relate to it: "Enhanced authorization includes data on internet protocol . . . additional data enriches our authorization decisions . . . our EBITDA is significantly impacted . . . when we prioritize our IT upgrade

decisions, we ought to give top priority to enhanced authorization data . . ."

> "Win-win is a frame
> of mind and heart
> that constantly seeks
> mutual benefit in all
> human interactions."
> —Stephen R. Covey

This kind of talk is an example of Expert Syndrome, the usually uncon-scious assumption that the audience knows what you're talking about. Just because you're an expert in something (and we're all experts in something), it doesn't mean other people are. "Quant" people (accountants, engi-neers, scientists, IT people) are often weak communicators because they live in a technical world and, understandably, have a hard time talking to people who don't live there.

Randy Olson is a biology professor turned filmmaker who had to learn how to communicate to nonspecialists. In his book *Don't Be Such a Scientist*, he tells techie people to lighten up on the expertise: "If you gather knowledge but are unable to convey it to others in a compelling form, you might as well not even have bothered."[19]

But it's not just the techies among us who get infected with Expert Syndrome. As we said, we're all experts in something. We all have jargon to spew. We all sometimes expect our listeners to read our minds. If your audience looks at you blankly, it could be *you* who is the clueless one.

What if you have people with different levels of knowl-edge and interest in your audience?

Some people will know more than others about your topic. Here's a simple way to meet everyone's needs: Briefly tell the whole story up front, then dive into the details. You'll serve those with low interest and attention span by giving them what they need first, while those with high interest will appreciate the deeper dive later.

In Tad's presentation, he dove straight into the deep water before telling his story. His goal was to sell racing suits; the buyers' goal was to win races. But he took no notice of the buyers' purpose. Instead, he went at it with these ends in mind:

- Sell the notion of our undersized suits.

- Elaborate on the increased permeability of our suits.

- Impress them with my knowledge.

And this was the result he got:

- Sent them to their smartphones.

Baffled by their response (or lack thereof), Tad went home. At first he asked himself, *Why weren't those people fascinated? I thought they were world-class experts—couldn't they see what a breakthrough the Missile is? They must be dumber than I thought.*

Later, in a more introspective mood, he thought, *What could I have done differently?* He was scheduled to give a presentation to a similar audience a few days later, so he decided to rethink his approach.

Win-Win—The Ultimate Connection

If Tad is smart, he will connect his purpose with his customers' purpose—and produce a joint purpose statement where everybody wins. When Tad analyzes his audience, who are buyers of equipment from the international ski racing community, his whole presentation changes:

ANALYZE YOUR AUDIENCE

WHAT DO THEY KNOW?

About the topic? A lot. They know the basics cold and they're generally familiar with the innovations in the industry. But they won't want to hear lectures. They'll want to know the bottom line, and they'll want to get to the point. In their place, so would I.

About you? We are competitive but not as big or famous as some other labels. We have a good track record but not a great one.

WHAT IS THEIR BIAS?

Toward the subject? They'd prefer to work with well-known, well-established brands, which they believe have more resources to create real competitive advantage.

WHAT ARE THEIR PRIORITIES?

Winning races

Winning races

Winning races

WHAT'S YOUR PURPOSE?

To sell my quota of our new ski-racing suit this fiscal year.

PURPOSE STATEMENT:

They will tend to win more races with our new ski-racing suit. We've proven it can make a skier as much as .7 percent faster on the downhill glide than any competitor's suit.

That's better. Like the rudder on a ship, the purpose statement determines the direction of the presentation; without the right rudder setting, the ship ends up where nobody wants to go. A little empathy on Tad's part should set him on the right course.

In Tad's original presentation, he was at the center of the story. He was the only winner. But in his new presentation, you (the listener) are now at the center of the story. *You* are winning. As Robert McKee advises, "Make those people the core character of a story that begins with *you*. And it's a big shift from talking in the first person, using first-person pronouns, to second-person pronouns. So stop talking about *me, I, us, we*—start talking about *you*." [20]

NOT THIS	THIS
"I-CENTERED"	"YOU-CENTERED"
Thanks for the opportunity to go over some of the features of our new product. I have just a few slides. From this slide you can see that the primary new feature of my Fissile Missile suit is...	You will win more races if you adopt my solution. In the ultracompetitive world of ski racing, you will stand out. You'll hit the finish line soonest...

In the new presentation, Tad talks about you, not about himself. You are in the foreground, he is in the background. By analyzing his audience, he now knows their priorities and he can put them first. The audience will know from the outset the answer to the question, "So what?"

The Job to Be Done

Your listeners are your customers. You're there to serve them. So what job are they hiring you to do for them? In any presentation you give, there's a big "so what?" question— and you've been hired to answer it. The sooner the better. In fact, your whole presentation should be an answer to a question worth asking.

So what big question do your listeners want you to answer for them?

That's why your audience analysis isn't finished until you anticipate the big questions they're going to ask you.

Tad's listeners wanted to know how he could help them win races. It was pretty much that simple. Of course, there would be other related questions as well (see next page).

Notice that Tad also anticipated a few questions he hoped they would *not* ask him. He would answer these questions in the presentation so they wouldn't become an obstacle later.

Try analyzing your audience. Who are they? What do they want to know? If you can anticipate the questions they'll ask, you can address them ahead of time in your presentation.

Tad could have taken questions throughout the presentation or after each key point; in a formal setting, he could announce that he will take questions only at the end. This time he decided to take questions throughout;

it would be a small audience, and he wanted to keep things informal and conversational.

By anticipating all these questions, Tad could design his presentation to meet the needs of his customers. In fact, the whole presentation could be built around these questions. It's to your advantage to anticipate and prepare for difficult or sensitive questions. After all, that's the job you've been hired to do.

Try analyzing your audience. What is their level of knowledge? How will you talk to different levels of knowledge? What are their priorities? How does your purpose connect to their priorities? What big question of theirs are

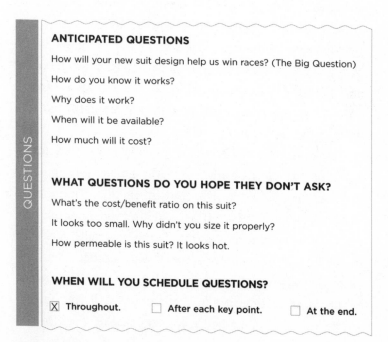

QUESTIONS

ANTICIPATED QUESTIONS

How will your new suit design help us win races? (The Big Question)

How do you know it works?

Why does it work?

When will it be available?

How much will it cost?

WHAT QUESTIONS DO YOU HOPE THEY DON'T ASK?

What's the cost/benefit ratio on this suit?

It looks too small. Why didn't you size it properly?

How permeable is this suit? It looks hot.

WHEN WILL YOU SCHEDULE QUESTIONS?

[X] Throughout.   ☐ After each key point.   ☐ At the end.

you answering? What questions can you anticipate? Can you build the answers to those questions into your presentation?

CONSIDER LOGISTICS

Before you go any further in planning your presentation, consider the logistics. You may be dealing not only with people sitting in front of you but also those participating via the internet or global conferencing—people peering at you on screens around the world.

Consider the time and place. When will it start? How long will you go? How many people will attend? What equipment will you need—Computer projector? Screen? Laptop or tablet or smartphone? Audio? Are you connecting people by web conference? How will you control the lights? Will you use low-tech equipment like charts or whiteboards and markers? It's best to get clear on these things as early as possible so you don't plan the wrong presentation for the wrong time, place, and people.

As you look at the logistics, anticipate how they might work against you. Thanks to all the fabulous technology that lets people everywhere join in, there are more risks than ever. What are these risks? Will there be other present-ers? Will you come early or late in the program? Will it be the middle of the night for some of your listeners? The end of the day when everyone's tired? Or right after lunch while people are digesting in a mental stupor? Will you be pre-senting online to an audience you could easily lose? Do you have the right audiovisual equipment? Do you have backup in case your equipment fails? What could happen if you ignore these risks?

In this part of the planner, you can think through potential logistical problems and make arrangements to minimize or eliminate those risks.

Try it yourself. Think through the logistics for your presentation. Small or big room? Is there plenty of equipment, or will you need to bring it? Will you need internet access? How many will be participating? In the room and around the world? What are the risks of giving a presentation in this situation? What can you do about them?

> develop

CONSIDER LOGISTICS

DATE/TIME

Date: Day of Week:

Time Allotted: Time of Day:

SETTING

☐ In Person   ☐ Web Meeting   ☐ Teleconference

☐ Hybrid   ☐ Other

Number of People: Special Needs:

Location: Internet Access:

Technology/Equipment:

RISKS

Other presenters?   Order (first, last)

Other:

DEVELOP STRONG KEY POINTS

Once you've planned your message, developed your purpose, and understand the audience, you are in position to determine the meat and potatoes of your presentation, with your goal always being to shift the knowledge and behavior of your audience.

"What do I say?" That's always a good question when you're planning a presentation. You might have a great top-level message in mind, a big idea to share, but what do you actually *say*?

The best way to develop the content for the body of your presentation is to brainstorm it. Remember, you already learned a lot by analyzing the audience, thinking about what they need to know, as well as questions they might ask, so you have a lot of content swirling around in your mind. Now we just need to get it out and get it organized.

There are three parts to an effective presentation: the introduction, the body, and the conclusion. We start with the body to get our most key compelling points out first. That will then guide us to create a very powerful introduction and conclusion.

Here are some brainstorming methods to try:

- Get all the thoughts out of your head on Post-its, tap it out on a keyboard, or use your thumbs on your smartphone—whatever's most comfortable for you.

- Talk as fast you can and record your voice, then transcribe it.

- Come up with as many ideas as you can, as fast as you can.

- Don't judge your ideas. Just record them as they come. If you're worried about saying dumb things, you might end up saying nothing at all.

- Imagine you're debating someone who thinks you're off base, and you have sixty seconds to defend your position. Record yourself.

- Start anywhere. You don't have to start at the beginning of your presentation.

Brain scientists now know that new insights come at moments like these. The "aha!" moment we often experience is accompanied by a "gamma spike"—a sudden flash of gamma-wave activity across the neocortex, the brain's creativity center. These gamma spikes happen at random, usually when you "let go" of the problem and just free-associate around it.[21] That's how rapid brainstorming works. With all the great information gathering you did already, your brain is ripe to synthesize and get your best ideas out—exactly what you need to support your purpose.

For his new presentation, Tad chose to write ideas rapidly on Post-it notes. The advantage of this approach is that he could group and arrange the notes when he finished brainstorming. See Tad's notes on the next page.

Features of New Missile Suit

Now Tad's job was to give these ideas some structure.

First, he put them into logical groups and gave a label to each group.

Missile Suit Faster Than Any Other Suit	**How We Know**	**Why? Enhanced Permeability**
.7 second average speed advantage	Wind tunnel, 7 liters more air over 250 m	7-11 liters total air flow enhancement
High correlation between permeability and drag, 11–17 m/s	2000 runs at Whistler, 500 at Cortina, 500 at Park City—250 m glide course	Undersizing cuts drag 7%
Hundredths of a second are a big deal	Analyzed speed using gps data	Zippers and seams raise permeability 2 liters/m²/sec
Loose fitting suits increase drag, vibration, lose .19 sec	Electron microscope	Cuts vibration over 100 km/h
		Texture = dimpled-knit sharkskin, 7 liters

Then he arranged the ideas in each group in an order that seemed logical to him: start with the data, tell how he got the data, and then explain the data (see his final order on the next page).

At last Tad had his ideas organized, and it took him only about a half hour to do this work. Although the details were technical, the presentation would be simple: His new racing suit was faster than any other suit, he could prove it was

Missile Suit Faster Than Any Other Suit	How We Know	Why? Enhanced Permeability
Hundredths of a second are a big deal	Wind tunnel, 7 liters more air over 250 m	7-11 liters total air flow enhancement
.7 second average speed advantage	Electron microscope	Undersizing cuts drag 7%
Loose fitting suits increase drag, vibration, lose .19 sec	2000 runs at Whistler, 500 at Cortina, 500 at Park City—250 m glide course	Texture = dimpled-knit sharkskin, 7 liters
High correlation between permeability and drag, 11-17 m/s	Analyzed speed using gps data	Zippers and seams raise permeability 2 liters/m²/sec
		Cuts vibration over 100 km/h

faster, and he could tell you why it was faster. This was all his listeners needed to shift their paradigm. Anything more would only clutter their brains, muddy the impact of the data, and delay a decision.

Try it yourself. Brainstorm your own ideas and then group them. Where do you see the connections among your ideas? Shoot for no more than three main groups, then arrange the ideas in order within each group. These groups will become the main topics of your presentation.

Three's the Charm

> develop

Why did Tad come up with *three* groups of ideas? Why not four or five or six?

Because he's smart. He knows the power of "three." Psychologists have found that, when you're trying to persuade someone, three claims are persuasive, two are often not enough, but four are too many. Professors Suzanne B. Shu and Kurt A. Carlson say, "More claims are better until the fourth claim, at which time [listeners] see all the claims with skepticism." The researchers call this effect the "charm of three," and suspect it has something to do with how much the average person can handle in short-term memory.[22]

Of course, great communicators have always known about the charm of three; that's why they often present three ideas, three main points, or three findings to support a claim. Lincoln spoke of "government of the people, by the people, and for the people." The French speak of "liberty, equality, and fraternity." Caesar said, "I came, I saw, I conquered." (Notice we just gave you three examples.)

> "No one can remember more than three points."
> —PHILIP CROSBY

Stories, songs, and jokes are full of threes ("Three guys walk into a bar . . ."). Naturalist Diane Ackerman reflects on this pattern: "We're so in love with patterns that we obsessively create our own, often in threesomes, such as morning, noon, and night; Macbeth's three weird sisters; the three wise men; ready, set, go; a sonata's three-part form; the genie's granting three wishes; small, medium, and large;

ABCs; Goldilocks and the three bears; the three little pigs; and so on. Three seems to be our pattern of choice."[23]

Remember, we said your presentation is in three parts; the intro, the body, and the conclusion. So now, you have three key points in the body to support your purpose. Now you decide what order to put them in.

Triple S Formula

How should you present your points?

We know that people remember the first and last things they hear. They also remember repeated information. The principle is simple: Make your point first *and* last—the repetition will help people remember and understand it.

We all know that memory is leaky, that we remember only bits and pieces of what we hear, and that a lot of what we think we remember is wrong. Psychologists say, "From perception to memory there are multiple opportunities for information to be incorrectly encoded"[24]—in other words, the audience just won't get it right unless you cut back on their opportunities to misunderstand you.

That means saying first what you want people to remember—and repeating it last. This gives the key points emphasis. You should also slow down and speak clearly when you deliver the key points. According to CUNY professor and expert in digital communication Cathy Davidson, "When you introduce the product at the beginning of the commercial and when you deliver the punch line at the end, your diction is much slower and your words are carefully e-nun-ci-a-ted."[25]

You should state each key point, support it, and summarize it. We call that the Triple S Formula.

Which of these two examples is easier to understand?

EXAMPLE 1: "The zippers and seams are placed to raise the permeability factor by about 2 liters per meter squared per second. Additionally, the suit is slightly undersized because force measurements are sensitive to suit size and make a difference of about 7 percent in aerodynamic drag, as this slide indicates. By undersizing we can enhance permeability by at least 2 liters and maybe more. But the real breakthrough is a textured, dimpled-knit sharkskin structure. Under an electronic microscope in the wind tunnel this structure appears to enable about 7 liters of additional permeability over a 250-meter glide course."

EXAMPLE 2: "The suit is designed to be about 11 liters more permeable than other suits on the market. Here's how it breaks down:

"We get 7 liters from our breakthrough design using textured, dimpled-knit sharkskin, which we proved using an electron microscope in a wind tunnel simulating a 250-meter glide course.

"We get 2 more liters by slightly undersizing the suit, which also cuts about 7 percent of the aerodynamic drag.

"And we get 2 more liters per meter squared per second by redesigning the zippers and seams.

"That adds up to 11 more liters of permeability than any other suit."

> develop

POINT 1

State: Here you state your point plainly.

Support: Here you provide enough supporting information to meet the needs of your audience. Some ideas for supporting information:

- Statistics

- Graphs and charts

- Examples

- Stories

- Personal experiences

- Expert opinions

- Definitions

- Explanations

Summarize: Here you re-state your point to reinforce it.

KEY POINTS

What did you notice that is different between the two versions?

Which one is more understandable? Why?

What purpose does summarizing serve?

Although the details are highly technical, most of us can follow Example 2 much better than Example 1. The key point comes up front ("you get 11 more liters of air with our suit"); then after three items of supporting data, the summary sentence ties the bow on the package.

Notice on page 71 how Tad used the planner tool to develop this key point.

The principle here is simple: Repeating a point makes it easier to remember. Through repetition you cement into

> develop

KEY POINTS

POINT 1

State: The suit is designed to be about 11 liters more permeable than other suits on the market.

Support:

- 7 liters from breakthrough design using textured, dimpled-knit sharkskin
- 2 more liters from undersizing
- 2 more liters from redesign of zippers and seams

Summarize: That adds up to 11 more liters of permeability than any other suit.

their brains the new insight, the "aha!" moment that shifts a paradigm. Professional persuaders are well aware of this principle; as Malcolm Gladwell says, "Understand what Nike and Coca-Cola understand: that if they can make their brands ubiquitous—if they can plaster them on billboards, on product displays inside grocery stores, on convenience-store windows, on the sides of buildings, on T-shirts and baseball caps, on the hoods and the roofs of racing cars, in colorful spreads in teen magazines—they can make their message impossible to ignore. The secret is not deception but repetition, not artful spinning but plain speaking."[26]

Your goal is to make your message impossible to ignore, to engage and reengage the brains of your listeners. You do that by stating, supporting, and summarizing each key point.

You can use this Triple S Formula in many communication situations, not just in a formal presentation. Use it when your boss asks you a question, when you're responding in a meeting, when you're on the phone with a client. The formula helps your listeners remember and understand your points.

In Amita's presentation, she told her buyers they would never have more or less inventory than they needed. She came up with three points to support that claim and used the Triple S Formula to plan out those points. (See how Amita's key points are broken out in the illustration that begins below.)

Amita is telling a convincing story of how her company differs from the typical manufacturer—instead of causing problems for her customers as the "others" do, she is solving them. And now she has three strong supporting points.

How about your presentation? Could you use the planner tool to come up with strong supporting points? Could you put them into the Triple S Formula, as Amita has done?

KEY POINTS

POINT 1

State: At Fissile, we distribute our own products and do not outsource this important function.

Support:

- Manufacturers usually hire a third party to distribute their products. As a result, they lose control of service quality.

- We control distribution, which means we get product to you when and where you need it.

- Our record shows we provide overnight deliveries and returns in 98 percent of cases.

Summarize: Because we distribute our own products, you never get stuck without the products you need or with inventory you don't need.

POINT 2

State: At Fissile, we make a science of inventory control.

Support:

- Manufacturers usually pass off inventory control to outsiders. As a result, they depend on others to know how much product they have on hand, and so on.

- We invest in our own inventory control system, tailored for us by the leading software developer in the industry.

- In the last three years we have achieved a 50% reduction in inventory adjustments. Our record for fulfilment time and backorders is the best in the business.

Summarize: Because we control our own inventory, we can virtually guarantee that you'll have access to exactly the product you want when you want it.

POINT 3

State: At Fissile, we make a science of forecasting product demand.

Support:

- Manufacturers vary in their ability to forecast how much product you'll need, which means you live with a lot of uncertainty.

- We don't have a crystal ball either, but we've invested significantly in forecasting software and processes.

- In the last three years we've been able to predict inventory turns at least 20% better than anyone else in our business. We give you access to an unprecedented twenty-six weeks of forecasts, so you can apply our knowledge to all your product lines. This means you don't have to grow any inventory beyond your needs.

Summarize: Because we are significantly better than anyone else in forecasting demand, all of your product lines can benefit from the knowledge we share.

CREATE A MEMORABLE INTRODUCTION AND CONCLUSION

You now have a clear main point supported by three key points—the meat of the sandwich. The bread is a memorable introduction and conclusion.

Now let's think about how to get the audience's attention right from the first with a memorable introduction.

Let's face it—the people sitting in front of you are jaded, cynical, and skeptical, but also curious. When you first stand to deliver, you've got to wipe out the skepticism and make the most of their curiosity. You've got to pull the rug out from under them, throw them off balance, and answer the "so what?" question. And because of the short attention span of your audience, you have 6.5 seconds to do all that!

This is not as tough as it sounds. Think about these presentation openers:

	NOT THIS	THIS
Peter, the finance guy	"I think this is a good time to go over some issues about credit card security. I have just a few slides."	"Who can tell me what this slide means? That's right ... we're losing a million dollars a year."

	NOT THIS	THIS
Flight attendant	"Ladies and gentlemen, please keep your seatbelts fastened until we reach the gate."	"Ladies and gentlemen, look out the window!"
Tad, the product director	"Thanks for the opportunity to go over some of the features of our new product."	"When thousandths of a second make the difference between a gold and a silver medal, you need every microsecond you can get."
Amita, the marketing director	"I'd like to explain how we have overhauled our inventory control system."	"You're fighting the inventory battle, and I'd like to show you how Fissile can help you win that battle in a big way."

What do you notice about the differences between the two columns? What do the effective openers have in common? What do the ineffective openers have in common?

Notice that the *This* column is all centered on the audience. The "you" pronoun dominates. The opposite is true of the *Not This* column: the pronouns that dominate are "I," "we," and "our." One way to tell if your presentation is effective or not is to count up the number of times you refer to yourself and compare it to the number of times you refer to your listeners. If your presentation is all "me-centered," you'll lose your listeners. But if you talk more about them than yourself, they'll stick with you.

Notice also that the *This* column is about the needs of the audience, not the needs of the presenter. There's an emotional appeal to the audience in each example: "*You're* fighting a battle . . . *you're* losing money . . . *you* need every microsecond you can get."

Some presenters resist making emotional appeals. "That's not businesslike," they say. Thoughtful people do require logical, rational reasons to act, but the emotional appeal needs to come first because of the way the human brain works. In order to persuade your audience to action, you must make them feel something. Remember the "do, know, feel" model.

> "In your first two minutes make at least one powerful statement and don't waste time on a long-winded introduction. Everyone knows why you are there and want to hear what you have to say—so get on with it."
> —TIMOTHY COOTE

The emotional brain (experts call it the limbic system) responds instantly to stimuli: a threat, a sudden danger, a surprising fact. Emotions are not irrational. They are instruments of life regulation. They contribute to our survival and well-being by providing us with a swift, automatic means to circumvent danger and take advantage of opportunities. Sharp emotions cause a sudden release of cortisol, a higher heart rate, quicker breathing.[27]

You want this kind of response from your audience, especially at first: "Oh my gosh, what should I do now?" Then you can safely appeal to the logical, reasoning part of their brains (the neocortex) with your data—and at that point they will start to plan, set priorities, and weigh the evidence.

Another reason you want to start with an emotional appeal is that people tend to remember best what comes first in a presentation. If they're emotionally charged up by the first thing they hear, they'll recall it better. Brain scientist John Medina says, "Emotionally charged events persist much longer in our memories and are recalled with greater accuracy than neutral memories."[28] You have to get their attention before you can hold on to it.

What have you seen or heard in presentations that got your attention? Let's think about some attention-getters you could try:

- Ask a question and let the audience members interact with you or with each other. Invite people to respond without putting anyone in particular on the spot. You might give people a minute to discuss your question before answering it.

- Ask a rhetorical question that doesn't require an answer but makes the audience think.

- Tell a quick story. A brief but relevant experience of your own grabs people's attention.

- Quote a testimonial. Share third-party stories that confirm your message.

- Show a striking visual—a graphic or a photo that sums up your message.

> develop

- Use a piece of art. Find a painting or a sculpture or even music that connects to your topic. Great art can inspire people to think differently about your subject.

- Use a prop, something that will make your presentation memorable. What object is unexpected, grabs the audience's attention, and ends up being entirely relevant?

- Share a startling fact, a piece of evidence that you know will intrigue your audience.

- Reverse expectations: "You thought I was going to talk about . . . but I'm really going to talk about . . ."

- Use humor—but make it brief, relevant, and definitely appropriate. Leave stale old jokes home.

Use your Presentation Planner to gain attention and state your purpose right up front.

INTRODUCTION

GAIN ATTENTION:

Do or say something that will immediately get your audience interested in what follows.

STATE YOUR PURPOSE:

Call your audience to action—tell them what you want them to do. Tell them what they need to know that will make them feel like doing what you want them to do.

> develop

> INTRODUCTION

Notice how the flight attendant used this formula:

GAIN ATTENTION:

"Ladies and gentlemen, look out the window! Do you see how fast we're going?"

STATE YOUR PURPOSE:

"When the pilot puts on the brakes, you're all going to fly down the aisle and smash your skulls on the bulkhead. Now get back in your seats and put your belts on!"

And that was all the flight attendant needed to do. End of presentation.

There was no need for anything else because she got the results she wanted immediately. In a way, this is the ideal presentation—she got their full attention and got them to do what she wanted without having to present a lot of supporting data.

Usually, you'll need to do more than that, but be aware that more information won't necessarily get you the results you want—if your Do-Know-Feel statement is strong enough, you might want to leave it at that.

In the following example, Amita gets attention by pulling the rug out from under her audience. They expected her to give them yet another product pitch, the sort of thing they constantly hear. Then they were surprised to hear her purpose statement—she was there to help them, to partner with them on a problem that kept them awake at night. This is how Amita escaped from the parade of "me too" product-pushers and made herself stand out in the customer's mind.

GAIN ATTENTION:

"Research shows that having too much inventory on your shelves costs you about a third of its value every year. On the other hand, having too little inventory hurts you, too. For every hour you're out of stock, you lose sales. You know how much out-of-stocks are costing you."

STATE YOUR PURPOSE:

"I'm not really here to talk about my products. Not today. You're fighting the inventory battle, and I'd like to show you how Fissile can help you win that battle in a big way."

Remember, every presentation you give is strategic. You'll either stand out or melt into the background. You'll either get results or be forgotten.

That's why a strong introduction is critical. It's how you set yourself apart from the rest. It doesn't have to be earth-shaking or spectacular—just ask a provocative question or tell a cool story to get your audience interested—but try to make it as distinctive as you can.

The introduction is so important, you'll need to practice it a few times. It creates the first impression. The more you practice the intro, the more quickly you'll be able to engage the audience.

Also, especially if your presentation is longer than the flight attendant's, you'll want to preview your key supporting points as Amita does here:

PREVIEW YOUR POINTS:

Lead-In Statement: We can help you win the battle of inventory because of three distinctive things we do.

Unlike most manufacturers, we:

1. Distribute our own products

2. Control our own inventory, and

3. Forecast demand better than anyone else.

Let me tell you about each of those things and why they're so important to your success.

A preview shows where you're going with your presentation, which helps the listening brain relax and focus. It also gives the audience a clear mental map of the road ahead.

Close with Power

People remember the beginning and end the most, so you want the end of the presentation to be powerful. A powerful conclusion motivates your audience to act on your purpose.

Great speeches and books are full of great endings:

- Winston Churchill: "Let us therefore brace ourselves to our duties, and so bear ourselves that, if the British Empire and its Commonwealth last for a thousand years, men will still say: 'This was their finest hour.'"

- Seneca: "As is a tale, so is life: It's not how long it is, but how good it is, that matters."

- Martin Luther King Jr.: "Free at last, free at last, thank God Almighty, we are free at last."

- Abraham Lincoln: "We here highly resolve . . . that government of the people, by the people, for the people, shall not perish from the earth."

- Amy Poehler: "Don't forget to tip your waitress."

The conclusion is the mirror image of your introduction:

CONCLUSION

IN CONCLUSION,

REVIEW YOUR POINTS:

Same three points from your presentation.

RESTATE YOUR PURPOSE:

Repeat your call to action—what do you want your audience to do?

CLOSE WITH POWER:

Repeat what you want the audience to know that will make them feel like doing what you want them to do.

See how Tad uses this formula to create a powerful close for his presentation:

CONCLUSION

IN CONCLUSION,

REVIEW YOUR POINTS:

"In summary, with our Fissile Missile suit, a racer gains on average—

- .4 seconds because of our dimpled-knit sharkskin
- .19 seconds by undersizing the suit
- .11 seconds because of changes to the seam design."

RESTATE YOUR PURPOSE:

"Through hundreds of tests, we've proven that our suit can make a ski racer .7 seconds faster on the downhill glide than any competitor suit, and on average you'll win more races if you adopt it."

CLOSE WITH POWER:

"Point-seven seconds might not sound like much, but when thousandths of a second make the difference between a gold and a silver medal, you need every microsecond you can get."

In his new presentation, Tad has succeeded in telling a compelling story about the search for a faster racing suit. He's told them about the exhausting, microscopic tests and the unexpected results from different fabrics and sizes of suit. But the story now has real relevance to the listeners—it's about helping them gain a competitive advantage they didn't have before.

Some people say there's too much repetition in the pattern we're teaching you. But if there's anything psychologists agree on, it's that people simply don't remember much of what they hear. Plus, especially in a longer, more complex presentation, people welcome a recap of key points. Johns Hopkins University cognitive psychology researcher Lisa Feigenson writes "A key signature of [working memory] is the severe constraint on the amount of information it can maintain at any given time."[29] In other words, nobody will remember what you said unless you stuff it repeatedly into their memories. Not to mention, we do this intuitively sometimes. Listen to yourself or others when they are making a long point or telling a story. Many times you will hear them say something like, "So as I said, I thought this would be a great way for us to reward the team." We almost feel the need to "tie the bow" on the package in people's minds.

Now, what about your presentation? How are you going to start? How will you end? Will people remember your call to action? Will they feel like doing it? Will they remember why they should do as you ask?

Assume that your listeners are going to another meeting where someone will ask them, "So, what was that presentation all about?"

Is this what will happen?

"He's a good guy. Knows his stuff."

"What did he say?"

"Something about permeable cloth. I didn't quite follow it, to be honest."

No, no, no.

You want your listeners to say: "He's built a racing suit that gives a nearly one-second advantage on the downhill."

"How does he know?"

"He's experimented with fabrics and sizing and seam designs—lots of things—and he did hundreds of tests. He even used an electron microscope to measure differences in drag. The upshot is you gain .7 seconds with his new suits. You know, when a few thousandths of a second make the difference between gold and silver, you need every micro-second you can get."

That's the best thing that can happen—when the listeners have not only bought in, but borrow your own words to say why.

Time Yourself

How long should you talk?

If you can get your message across as fast as our Las Vegas flight attendant did, a few seconds are enough. Obviously, some presentations require more time than others, and the amount of time you take really depends on the situation.

But ideally, you should try not to take more than eighteen to twenty minutes. Chris Anderson, the founder of the wildly popular TED Talks, was asked, "Why are the talks only eighteen minutes?" He responded, "It's long enough to be serious and short enough to hold people's attention. It turns out that this length also works incredibly well online. It's the length of a coffee break."[30]

And then of course we have many presentations that will last an hour or more if necessary. Follow the methods to "skinny" the content down so you get your point across and then have enough time to engage your audience in a question-and-answer session. Interactivity is a great "con-nect." No matter how long the presentation, keep this rule of thumb in mind: *Spend about 10 percent of your time on your*

> develop

introduction, 10 percent on your conclusion, and 80 percent on the body of your presentation.

Make a Script

The Presentation Planner is a great thinking tool for developing a tight, persuasive, memorable presentation. Sometimes the planner is all you need—having done the mental work, you're ready to go. Other people like to use the planner to create a script of the whole presentation. That's what Amita decided to do in order to prepare better—a very good idea! You can see her presentation here.

GAIN ATTENTION:

"Research shows that having too much inventory on your shelves costs you about a third of its value every year. On the other hand, having too little inventory hurts you, too. For every hour you're out of stock, you lose sales. You know how much out-of-stocks are costing you."

STATE YOUR PURPOSE:

"I'm not really here to talk about my products. Not today. You're fighting the inventory battle, and I'd like to show you how Fissile can help you win that battle in a big way."

PREVIEW YOUR POINTS:

"We can help you win the battle of inventory because of three distinctive things we do. Unlike most manufacturers, we:

- Distribute our own products

- Control our own inventory, and

- Forecast demand better than anyone else."

INTRODUCTION

POINT 1

State: At Fissile, we distribute our own products and do not outsource this important function.

Support:

- Manufacturers usually hire a third party to distribute their products. As a result, they lose control of service quality.

- We control distribution, which means we get product to you when and where you need it.

- Our record shows we provide overnight deliveries and returns in 98 percent of cases.

Summarize: Because we distribute our own products, you never get stuck without the products you need or with inventory you don't need.

POINT 2

State: At Fissile, we make a science of inventory control.

Support:

- Manufacturers usually pass off inventory control to outsiders. As a result, they depend on others to know how much product they have on hand, and so on.

- We invest in our own inventory control system, tailored for us by the leading software developer in the industry.

- In the last three years we have achieved a 50% reduction in inventory adjustments. Our record for fulfilment time and backorders is the best in the business.

Summarize: Because we control our own inventory, we can virtually guarantee that you'll have access to exactly the product you want when you want it.

POINT 3

State: At Fissile, we make a science of forecasting product demand.

Support:

- Manufacturers vary in their ability to forecast how much product you'll need, which means you live with a lot of uncertainty.

- We don't have a crystal ball either, but we've invested significantly in forecasting software and processes.

- In the last three years we've been able to predict inventory turns at least 20% better than anyone else in our business. We give you access to an unprecedented twenty-six weeks of forecasts, so you can apply our knowledge to all your product lines. This means you don't have to grow any inventory beyond your needs.

Summarize: Because we are significantly better than anyone else in forecasting demand, all of your product lines can benefit from the knowledge we share.

IN CONCLUSION,

REVIEW YOUR POINTS:

In summary, we:

1. Distribute our own products

2. Control our own inventory, and

3. Forecast demand better than anyone else.

RESTATE YOUR PURPOSE:

As I've said, at Fissile we can help you win the inventory battle in a big way.

CLOSE WITH POWER:

"We can make sure you have exactly the right amount of product that you'll need at any moment—no more, no less. What does that mean to you? Saving a third of the value you would otherwise lose on overstocks, and saving the sales you would lose on out-of-stocks."

DEVELOPING A VIRTUAL PRESENTATION

If you're giving a presentation online, a lot of the guidance we've already given you still applies. You still need a strong purpose statement (Do-Know-Feel), strong supporting points, and a strong introduction and close. But because the audience is far away behind a screen, you have to engage and reengage continually. How do you keep them off email when you can't look them in the eye? How do you stop them from playing with the dog while you're talking?

For virtual presentations, everything we've said goes double: Getting attention with a great intro, riveting key points and evidence, and above all answering the big question, "So what?"

> "You must engage your audience and hold them 'virtually accountable' for what they see, hear, and do."[31]
> —FRANKLINCOVEY AUTHORS TREION MULLER AND MATT MURDOCH

Here are a few guidelines to keep in mind for virtual presentations.

Plan Your Message

- Solicit questions after each key point.
- Allow the audience to ask questions verbally and through chat pods.
- Keep virtual presentations under sixty minutes when possible.

Develop Your Message

- Use a poll as a virtual attention getter.

- Establish credibility with a brief bio.

- Explain the features of the platform at the outset so they know how to interact with you.

- Use impactful questions to keep the audience engaged ("How does this strategy relate to our goal?" or "What obstacles do you expect to encounter?").

- Design a final poll or chat to act as a call to action.

››› *Practice Idea*

Spend the next few minutes practicing your presentation using the planner you filled out. Stand up and go find a wall you really like. Give your presentation to the wall three times, imagining your real audience. For now, work on the flow and structure.

How did that go? Did you notice differences between your first time and your third? Did you find yourself making changes to your words? The third one probably started to flow more smoothly. If you are like most people, what looks good on paper may not work so well when you start to actually hear them come out of you. Verbalizing what you write is a key part of the design process. Saying your presentation a few times as practice goes a long way to getting exactly what you need to change people's paradigms.

In the next chapter we will consider the visuals you will use in your presentation.

TO SUM UP ⓘ

Your message is powerful only if it answers the "so what?" question that is on the mind of everyone in your audience.

To serve them well, you need to shift a paradigm that isn't working for them. Like the flight attendant who got everyone back in their seats, tell them what they need to know that will make them feel like doing what they *should* do—instead of what they *are* doing.

Now that you've developed a powerful, well-organized message, let's move on to the next step: designing impactful visuals that help the audience *see* what you mean.

> develop

Presentation Planner

Use this Presentation Planner tool to develop your message.

ANALYZE YOUR AUDIENCE

WHAT DO THEY KNOW?

About the topic?

About you?

WHAT IS THEIR BIAS?

Toward the subject?

WHAT ARE THEIR PRIORITIES?

WHAT'S YOUR PURPOSE?

PURPOSE STATEMENT:

QUESTIONS

ANTICIPATED QUESTIONS

WHAT QUESTIONS DO YOU HOPE THEY DON'T ASK?

WHEN WILL YOU SCHEDULE QUESTIONS?

☐ Throughout.   ☐ After each key point.   ☐ At the end.

CONSIDER LOGISTICS

DATE/TIME

Date: Day of Week:

Time Allotted: Time of Day:

SETTING

☐ In Person ☐ Web Meeting   ☐ Teleconference

☐ Hybrid   ☐ Other

Number of People: Special Needs:

Location: Internet Access:

Technology/Equipment:

RISKS

Other presenters?   Order (first, last)

Other:

GAIN ATTENTION:

STATE YOUR PURPOSE:

PREVIEW YOUR POINTS:

Lead-In Statement:

    1.

    2.

    3.

INTRODUCTION

> develop

KEY POINTS

POINT 1

State:

Support:

Summarize:

POINT 2

State:

Support:

Summarize:

POINT 3

State:

Support:

Summarize:

CONCLUSION

**IN CONCLUSION,
REVIEW YOUR POINTS:**

1.

2.

3.

RESTATE YOUR PURPOSE:

CLOSE WITH POWER:

CHAPTER 3

DESIGN IMPACTFUL VISUALS

K IP, THE FULFILLMENT GUY, LOOKED around
the boardroom with satisfaction. In a few minutes a meeting of the board of directors would
start, and he was ready to give his presentation. At eight
of the ten seats he had placed a box, the sort of package
customers get when they order products from Fissile Co.
Seven of the boxes were pristine, but the eighth one was
different—it was ripped and dirty. And two seats had no
boxes.

As the board members wandered in, they picked up the boxes and shook them like kids at a birthday party. "For us?" they asked.

"Yes indeed!" Kip said, as he greeted and shook hands with everyone. "But please don't open them yet."

The two people without boxes peeked questioningly at each other. "What's going on?" they whispered. "Why didn't we get one?"

The chairperson, a famous winter athlete with sun-streaked hair and the look of a competitor, was the last to arrive. She bustled in, took her seat, and stared at the crushed box in front of her.

"What's this?"

"A present for you," Kip smiled. The chairperson glanced around at the other boxes, which looked fine.

"Mine's a little different from the others, isn't it?"

"Yes it is," Kip answered. "Please, everyone, open your presents!"

> "Show the readers everything; tell them nothing."
> —ERNEST HEMINGWAY

They broke into the boxes and pulled out beautiful pairs of winter gloves. Attached to each glove was a tiny metallic label with the board member's name and contact information on it.

"This is our new product—personalized ski gloves, and we've provided a free pair for each member of Fissile Co.'s board of directors," Kip announced proudly. "Who here has ever lost a glove on the slopes?"

All skiers, the board members chuckled and raised their hands.

"Well, now if someone finds your glove, they'll be able to return it to you. What do you think?"

"What about us?" the two who had no gloves asked.

"Oh, yours didn't arrive on time. Sorry."

And then all eyes turned to the chairperson, who was holding up a pair of gloves obviously meant for a child. Everyone laughed.

"So what's this?" she asked, a little miffed.

"Oops. Wrong size! And, um, sorry about the battered box. Those things happen, you know. They *shouldn't*, but they *do*."

Then Kip flicked on the projector. On the screen was a video clip of a frowning young man holding up a new ski suit that was many sizes too small for him. His complaint was, shall we say, vocal.

"I'm Jack Yabu and I'm one of your customers. I paid $800 for your Fissile Missile Mark One racing suit. I gave you all my information and did it right. But what did I get? This child-sized Fissile Whistle Beginner's suit, price $90. So how am I supposed to race in this?"

> "One picture is worth a thousand words."
> —CHINESE PROVERB (maybe)

Kip put up another photo. It was a dad with two sad-looking young daughters.

"Hi, we're the Whitakers. These are my daughters Sara and Sonia. A month before Christmas I ordered skis for my kids, but they never arrived. We still don't know what happened . . ."

>> design

This was the next slide:

"One-third," Kip said. "That's the number I want you to remember. Fully one-third of our holiday orders this year had problems. Express boxes were damaged, wrong products delivered, or delivered late, or *never* delivered. Customers were furious.

"As fulfillment manager for Fissile, I find this appalling. That's why I'm proposing we drop our fulfillment service provider and bring all fulfillment in house. I'm saying we should deliver our own products instead of depending on somebody else to do it."

What do you think of Kip's presentation so far?

Kip has a big job on his hands. He's in charge of warehousing and packaging and getting the right products to the right people at the right time. This is called the "fulfillment" process, and his company has always used a third party to provide this service.

So Kip's job up till now has been to try and get the service provider to do the job right and then to take calls from upset customers when the provider messed up. He was up to his neck in complaints, and he was convinced he could do the job by himself better than the provider could.

But now he had to convince the board of directors that he could do the job. It had been a board decision in the first place to go with the third party because they thought it would be cheaper and less hassle. So the task at hand was to *change a paradigm.*

It's a strong paradigm. Many large companies that don't want the expense and trouble of delivering their own products outsource fulfillment to companies that specialize in it. It makes sense for many companies, but in Kip's opinion, not for *his* company.

How do you think Kip is doing at changing that paradigm?

As Hemingway advised, Kip is showing the problem to the audience instead of telling them about it.

Usually, we think of a presentation as "tell-tell-tell."

Actually, it's better to think of a presentation as "show-show-show."

Why?

Because, as we all intuitively know and as every expert on the subject will tell you, pictures are generally more impactful than words. In a famous experiment years ago, researchers showed people ten thousand pictures and found they had amazing recall for the pictures but not for the accompanying text.

The study concluded that "pictorial memory is quantitatively superior to verbal memory,"[32] which is just a fancy way to say that people remember pictures better than words. (Most of us have heard the Chinese proverb, "One picture is worth a thousand words." Some have suggested the proverb did not actually come from China but from advertising guru Fred Barnard, who called it a Chinese proverb "so that people would take it seriously." Wherever it came from, it's a serious principle.)

> "As the Chinese say,
> 1,001 words are worth
> more than a picture."
> —JOHN MCCARTHY

So make your message visual. Create pictures that will have an emotional impact on the audience, pictures they will remember long after they've forgotten what you said.

Unfortunately, in our experience, most presentations are visual disasters. Usually, we get to see—

- Slides full of bullet points we'll never remember
- Spreadsheets we can't even read
- Fonts so tiny we feel like we're taking an eye test
- Obnoxious colors ("Those red letters are buzzing!")
- Mysterious charts and graphs ("What do all those numbers even mean?")

- Irrelevant pictures ("Why am I looking at
  a photo of a duck in a presentation on last
  quarter's financials?")

Once we saw a financial report delivered on PowerPoint slides in front of a high-powered executive audience. In the upper left corner of every slide was a picture of a floating duck. When it was over and we were about to leave, somebody finally asked the presenter, "Why the duck?"

The presenter said, "Oh . . . I forgot to say. It's to show that we're all working hard but keeping our cool. You know . . . like a duck paddling like mad under water but calm and collected on the surface?"

Cute. A few groans and snickers and we were out of there.

This kind of silliness aside, most people aren't sure how to make a presentation with visual impact. For instance, if Kip had given a typical presentation, it probably would've gone like this:

	A	B	C	D	E
1	Order ID	OrderDate	TargetDate	DeliveryDate	OrderStatus
2	12123	5/18/2013 15:45:46	5/21/2013 15:45:46	5/26/2013 12:12:23	Past Due
3	12124	6/7/2013 18:38:34	6/19/2013 18:38:34	6/9/2013 11:23:56	Target Met
4	12126	6/7/2013 15:45:46	6/18/2013 15:45:46	6/18/2013 16:20:00	Past Due
5	11231	6/7/2013 10:28:58	6/15/2013 10:28:58	6/15/2013 13:00:00	Past Due
6	13211	5/18/2013 15:45:46	5/22/2013 15:45:46	5/23/2013 12:00:00	Past Due
7	11226	5/29/2013 13:21:46	6/2/2013 13:21:46	6/1/2013 00:00:00	Target Met
8	10123	6/8/2013 10:14:34	6/13/2013 10:14:34	6/13/2013 00:00:00	Target Met

design

KIP: I just want to thank the board for the chance to take just a few minutes and talk about the problems we're having with fulfillment. If it's okay I'd like to show just a few slides.

"This is part of the readout on December's product deliveries. We did pretty well for most of the season, but you can see here and here . . . Oh, I guess you can't see that very well . . . Anyway, here you can see that in several cases the order configuration was entered properly but the delivery data don't align. What we think's going on is that the pick-and-pack process our provider is operating with doesn't meet standard, and the result is a lot of mixed-up deliveries.

"Now, my primary concern is their order-entry system. It's fully automated, but for an operation our size a manual system would be just as good if not better, I think, and would serve our brand better. The one thing they have that would be hard for us to reproduce is, naturally, the tracking system for shipping notification . . ."

And of course by this time, while Kip is talking to himself and his spreadsheet, some board members are checking their phones, others are lost in the fog, and the rest are wondering what's for lunch.

"If your mother likes your drawing of a duck and hangs it on the refrigerator, that doesn't mean it's good."
—MICHAEL THOMAS FORD

But Kip knew better. He was a natural talker, a high-energy person, but his personality wouldn't have saved him if he didn't know how to connect with his audience visually. A spreadsheet covered with tiny figures is *not* the way to do it (spreadsheets are for handouts, not for slides).

Instead, Kip reproduced for the board members the same lousy *experience* that so many of Fissile's customers were having. While some people were happy about their nice new gloves, three of the ten were very unhappy about getting nailed. The videos of actual unhappy customers tapped the nail in further, and the gigantic fraction "1/3" hit the nail right on the head.

Now, that's impact. And paradigms don't move without a solid impact.

Experts call this sort of presentation "visual-auditory-kinesthetic," meaning you can see, hear, and touch *reality*, instead of listening to a droning voice and pretending to look at boring slides. A master presenter, Kip knew that if his audience could see and hear and feel their customers' pain, their paradigms would change.

Now, getting the gloves customized and packaged, the videos shot, and the scene set took a lot of work, but then a lot was at stake for Kip: *his job*. He refused to be a victim of the board's paradigm. He resolved to change it, and he knew it would take some doing. So he prepared carefully.

Not all presentations require this intense preparation, but Kip's is a great example of the principles of good visual design.

If you want to be an impactful presenter, here are three key principles to follow when designing your visual message:

The Principle of Impact

- Use relevant images
- Provide visual variety
- Use high-quality images

>> design

The Principle of Pattern

- Apply a visual theme
- Use color to create interest
- Be choosy about fonts

The Principle of Simplicity

- Eliminate visual clutter
- Keep text to a minimum
- Limit builds and transitions

IMPACT

Think of the images you've seen in your life that have stuck with you and maybe changed you.

Think about your parents' wedding pictures or the video you shot at the birth of your child.

What about memorable images from your favorite movies or a great vacation?

And what about those horrific images that unfortunately make up our landscape from time to time? Images of catastrophes and tragedies that unleash a torrent of thought and emotions.

Pictures can have strong, immediate impact that words can't match. A strong image has the power not only to shift a paradigm but also to smack it hard and even reverse it. Kip's videos of actual unhappy customers made that kind of an impression on the board of directors.

If you're going to knock paradigms around, you need to remember the principle of *emotional impact*. Ultimately, it's how people feel that dictates what they do; and if you want them to change their behavior, give them a picture that will move their emotions.

Here are three tips for making your presentation visually impactful:

- Use relevant images
- Provide visual variety
- Use high-quality images

Use Relevant Images

So the projector or screen is set up, you're all wired—or Wi-Fi'd—and you're ready to go. What's the first image you want your audience to see?

The word "WELCOME" in big letters?

The title of your presentation with a big logo?

Your cat (by mistake)?

Of course, none of these first-impression images are *wrong*, just useless. Think about the impact you want to make *from the beginning*.

> "Of all of our inventions for mass communication, pictures still speak the most universally understood language."
> —WALT DISNEY

What were the first images the audience saw in Kip's presentation?

>> design

For some, a box with a gift inside. For one person, a broken box with the wrong gift. For others, no box. Videos of ill-fated customers. A giant "1/3." All of these images added up to give Kip's audience a smack in the paradigm.

CREATE PARADIGM-BUSTING VISUALS

If you really want to connect with your audience and move that paradigm, you've got to start with the most relevant image that will, as the saying goes, "knock their socks off."

Usually, it's the visualization of your main point from your Presentation Planner. That main point was crafted to give people the information (Know) that will motivate them (Feel) to act (Do). Is there a way to picture that main point for them?

In Dr. Jill Bolte Taylor's "My Stroke of Insight," always voted one of the top two or three TED Talks, she starts with a moving photo of herself with her brother, who suffers from schizophrenia. The picture makes clear the personal stake she has in her brain research and strikes a strong emotional chord with the audience.

> "Pictures cannot be accessories to the story—they have to contain the story."
> —TATJANA SOLI

At the start of another of the most popular TED Talks, Simon Sinek draws on a chart a simple diagram he calls the Golden Circle of Innovation. No high-tech visual stuff, not even PowerPoint slides. Just a piece of chart paper and a couple of markers. But his whole powerful insight is summed up in that one image.

So when you start to present, is the visual impression "Meh" or "Wow!"? Will people sit up and feel something, or will they sit back and check out?

CREATE A "BIG-PICTURE PICTURE"

As you develop your message, you should be thinking, "What image will make the most impact up front? What image sums up the emotional impact of my presentation? How can I turn the strategic point of my presentation into a picture?"

The answer is what experts call the "primary graphic" or "macrovisual." It shows the key points or the major theme you want to get across to your audience. It's the whole story in a picture. It's the one graph or chart or photo or illustration or number that sends paradigms spinning. We call it "the Big-Picture Picture."

One evening, two businessmen, Rollin and Herb, were having dinner in a San Antonio restaurant. Rollin grabbed a napkin and drew this picture for Herb.

Rollin explained that you couldn't take a plane from one of these booming Texas cities directly to the other. You had to go through various airline hubs. For example, to get from Houston to Dallas, you had to fly to Denver, turn around, and come back; and to get to San Antonio from Houston, you had to go through Chicago! What if there were a small, inexpensive airline that flew only to the three points on the napkin?

This was a Big-Picture Picture. Rollin King and Herb Kelleher used the picture on this napkin to get the investment they needed, and Southwest Airlines was born—one of the most profitable airlines in history.

Remember the presentation given by Peter, the finance guy?

PETER: "Who can tell me what this slide means?"

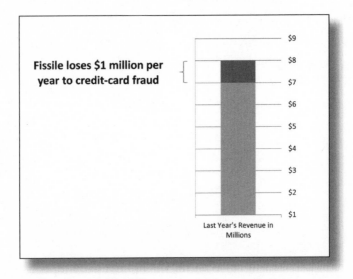

AMITA (the marketing person): *Ohmygosh, we lost a million dollars this year!*

Peter got this reaction by starting with a macrovisual, a primary visual—a Big-Picture Picture, the picture that changes paradigms.

What pictures have changed your paradigms?

The Big-Picture Picture:

- Simplifies everything
- Shifts paradigms
- Sums up the whole point of the presentation
- Often shows a major contrast (before/after, now/then, this/not this)
- Makes people feel like doing what you want them to do

The Big-Picture Picture is the *most relevant image* the audience needs to see. It's the big "so what?" Sometimes the Big-Picture Picture is the only picture you need to show them. If there's one thing you want them to remember, it's that image. You want it burned into their brains.

And if you can't use a real picture, paint a word picture. Remember the flight attendant who told everyone to look out the window, then depicted what would happen to them if the plane had to stop?

Use the Big-Picture Picture—

- At the beginning of the presentation for a powerful "grabber"
- At the end of the presentation for a powerful close

>> design

So what's the Big-Picture Picture for your presentation? What do you want them to see first and last?

PROVIDE VISUAL VARIETY

One of the first things Steve Jobs did when he took over Apple was to ban PowerPoint. "I hate the way people use slide presentations instead of thinking. People would confront a problem by creating a presentation. I wanted them to engage, to hash things out at the table, rather than show a bunch of slides."[33]

We wouldn't go so far as to ban PowerPoint. It can be a useful tool. But why do you think Steve Jobs, a remarkable business thinker if there ever was one, reacted so strongly to presentation slides?

Because the slides had stopped being thinking tools. Slides had taken the place of real conversation. Slides had become a crutch for a lecturer, speaker notes for one-way communication.

> "People come to a conclusion about your presentation by the time you're on the second slide. After that, it's often too late for your bullet points to do you much good."
> —SETH GODIN

Who hasn't been bored or hypnotized or practically put into a coma from watching endless PowerPoint slides filled with bulleted text? A friend of ours calls it "death by bullet points."

Of course, there's nothing wrong with bullet points. They're useful if you really want to show us an important list and only a list will do the job. But we don't need to see your bulleted speaker notes. Today we don't want a lecture, we want to think and talk together with you. That means your slides need to be thinking tools.

Here are some ideas for using visuals to generate thinking:

1. **Use a variety of visuals as conversation starters.** Pictures raise questions, evoke strong emotions, and kick off debates. How many times do you see this phrase on the internet?

   "This picture will make you . . ."

   (Cry, question, think, cringe, change your mind, throw up, want to lose weight, etc.)

2. **Use visuals to create suspense.** When Kip put the big 1/3 ratio on the screen all by itself (see page 100), people naturally wondered what it meant (and why it was so big).

3. **Use visuals to tell stories.** If you can get them, show pictures of the real people, places, and events in your stories. Use stock photos only if you can't get the real ones. Better yet, use brief video clips.

   Take a lesson from Kickstarter, the wildly successful source for crowdfunding. Its whole purpose is to convince people to invest their money in new ideas. So what's the best way to do that? By telling a compelling story on video.

   Content marketer Shane Snow explains the importance of stories to Kickstarter: "The reason

Kickstarter works, and how thousands of creators have rallied the support of millions on its platform, is because it allows people to get their stories in front of others. And it doesn't just allow it; Kickstarter requires it. Every project must have a video where the creators explain why they're doing what they're doing and why they need help. Unfortunately, in the era of PowerPoint, many of us have forgotten how to tell a good story."[34]

4. **Use the right visual for your purpose.** Think of graphics as tools for doing specific jobs. (See the options beginning on page 115.) What job needs to be done?

> "There are few styles of speaking more stultifying than the modern slide-driven presentation."
> —MAX ATKINSON

Choose the right visual for the job you want to do.

Next, how do you know if your visual is any good? It's good if it will get people thinking and talking and acting. If it won't do that, skip it.

>> design

DO YOU WANT TO . . .	THEN USE A . . .
Show percentages?	Pie chart 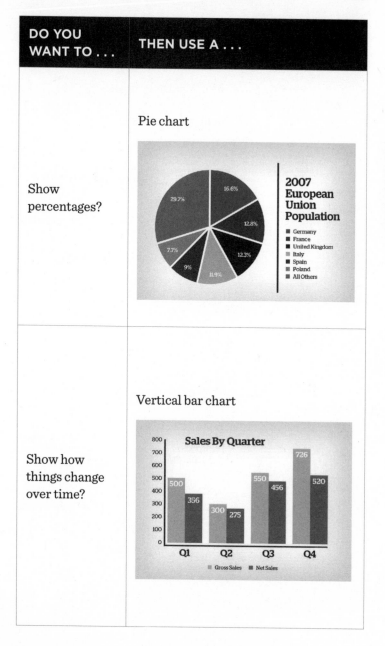
Show how things change over time?	Vertical bar chart

DO YOU WANT TO . . .	THEN USE A . . .
Compare numbers?	Horizontal bar chart 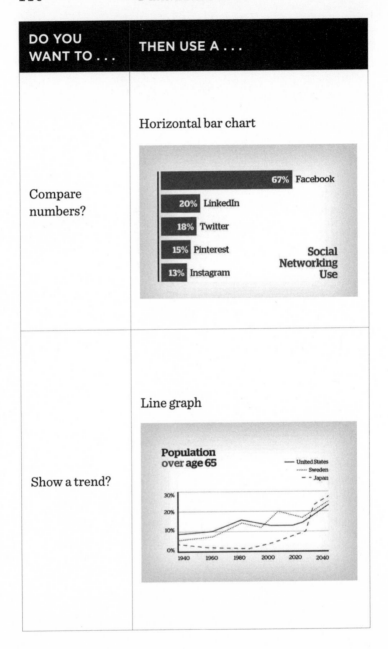
Show a trend?	Line graph

>> design

DO YOU WANT TO . . .	THEN USE A . . .
Show the steps in a process?	**Flow chart**
Show how a company is organized?	**Organization chart**

USE HIGH-QUALITY IMAGES

When we say use a "high quality" image, we don't just mean high-def photos and slick graphics. We mean something far more than that.

How do you define quality? Here's how we define it: If it does the job it's supposed to do, then it's quality.

For example, Ana was a product manager worried about the shrinking sales of her product. She desperately wanted the company to invest in an upgrade because she believed there was huge untapped potential for it, but she was competing for budget with other big projects. Unfortunately, Ana wasn't very skilled at presenting a case, and she went into the executive meeting with this slide that showed how her product was slipping in the market:

System Integrators' Product Sales

	LAUNCH	YEAR 1	YEAR 2	YEAR 3	YEAR 4
1,200,000					
1,100,000		1,050,000			
1,000,000					
900,000					
800,000			860,000		
700,000	750,000				
600,000				600,000	
500,000					
400,000					450,000
300,000					
200,000					
100,000					

Well, the executive team had seen this sort of thing countless times. "It only represents 5 percent of the business," they said. "Products have a life cycle," they said. "We have other priorities," they said. "It had a good run . . . maybe it's time for this one to die," they said.

This visual failed the quality test—not only because it was a spreadsheet and difficult to make out, but also because it just *didn't do the job* Ana needed to do.

But Ana didn't give up. She did more homework and created a much more impactful slide.

The new slide argued that her product could go from 5 percent of the company's revenues to 40 percent with an upgrade. With the strong evidence she had, the new slide did the trick, and she got her budget.

That's why it was a "high-quality" visual: It did the job it was supposed to do, and did it well. The new slide is simple and clean, but more important, it makes the point Ana really needs to make.

PATTERN

The principle of a pattern is simple: People learn and understand better from an organized presentation than from a disorganized one. It's the opposite of ODTAA, which is the problem with so many poor presentations where the visuals become more mess than message.

"People learn better when cues that highlight the organization of the material are added."
—Richard Mayer

There are all kinds of visual ODTAA in a world where people design their own presentations. There's the "bullet-riddled corpse," which is just one bullet list after another. There's the "photomaniac," whose slides are filled with photos that go on and on and on. Then there's the "fontaholic," who tries out every possible typeface.[35] And so on.

Your audience needs a predictable pattern in your visuals so they can grasp your message easily. Here are some tips:

- Apply a visual theme.
- Use color to create interest.
- Be choosy about fonts.

Apply a Visual Theme

Create a consistent look and feel across all your slides. To do this, avoid using PowerPoint templates that restrict your choices. Instead, create your own pattern of headings and colors, and use coordinating colors and a matching background. Let's break this down:

Use headings to communicate the structure of your presentation. Too many slide presentations float by the audience like a stream of debris. Even a well-organized presentation can seem shapeless and messy if the structure of the message is not clearly visible.

Preview key points. If you have three points to make, but viewers never see the three points displayed, they might not get them. So create slides to preview your three key points from your Presentation Planner.

For Ana, persuading the executive team to upgrade her product meant "burning into their brains" three main reasons for the upgrade, so she created three big slides—one for each reason—and presented them in order of importance to her audience:

>> design

2

Strengthen Brand and Reputation

System **Integrators**

3

"Delight Our Customers"

System **Integrators**

By previewing her key points in this way, Ana gave structure to her argument. Her end in mind: for every board member to leave the room mumbling these three key points.

In a long presentation, you want to use overview slides like these to introduce and to sum up each section so your listeners stay oriented. Keep the section title in a header on each slide so viewers always know where they are in relation to the presentation as a whole.

Of course, Ana could have loaded all her reasons for the upgrade onto one big text slide. Here they are, in no particular order and with no way to tell which reasons were more important:

>> design

Why Should We Update This Product

- We need to grow this product that was started four years ago.
- Our competitors are really taking the lead and we are falling behind.
- We were known for quality, and I'm not sure this is our reputation today.
- Companies are spending millions in this product line and we are missing out.
- Our brand is jeopardized and we are not being seen as innovative.
- Our ratings with the reviewers are dropping as we speak.
- We are violating our company values, and we need to change that.
- We are not delighting our customers, and that is a problem we need to solve.

This ODTAA slide is both unimpactful and disorganized. You can't get your head around it because there's no pattern to it.

Use bullets sparingly. Bullets are useful for making lists, and sometimes a list is just what you need, like when you're previewing your key points or itemizing the parts of a machine. But long lists of bullets are hard for your audience. People can't remember long lists. Everything looks the same, so it's hard to tell which items take priority. Important information can get lost in bullet lists.

Try not to use more than three to five bullets in a list. Better yet, turn your list into a graphic (see graphic on the next page).

Don't use bullets if numbers work better. Use numbers for steps in a process or listing things in order of importance.

Don't do this:

The 5 Choices to Extraordinary Productivity

• Act On the Important, Don't React to the Urgent
• Go for Extraordinary, Don't Settle for Ordinary
• Schedule the Big Rocks, Don't Sort Gravel
• Rule your Technology, Don't Let It Rule You
• Fuel Your Fire Don't Burn Out

• Decisions
• Attention
• Energy

Do this:

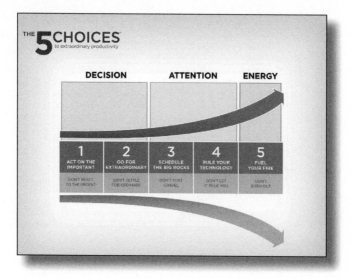

Use Color to Create Interest

Here are some tips for using color to generate interest:

Use color to focus attention. Color helps you control where the eyes go. For example, use bright colors to focus the eye on important information and dimmer colors for less important stuff.

In the slide on page 126, Ana used color to draw attention to the key point. The bright white arrow on a dimmer background focuses the audience on the fact that sales are falling.

Use background and lettering that fits your environment. Most presenters use a light background and dark letters.

Some believe a dark background with light letters is more dramatic and easier on the eyes, as in the slide on the next page. (But if you know your slides will be printed, use dark letters on a white background—people will thank you for saving ink!)

Also consider the room you're presenting in. If the light is low, a dark background might be best (you won't blind people), while bright colors on a white background might work better in a well-lit room.

Use bright colors for energy. While lots of color can be jarring, it can also bring energy to your presentation. Though it's presented here in black and white, you can imagine how the color combination in the "Delight" slide (see bottom of the next page) is lively and still draws the focus of the audience to the bright key word "Delight".

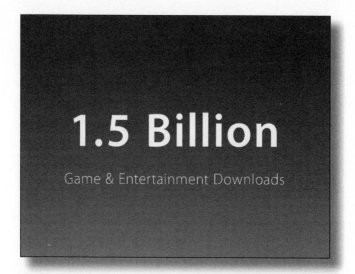

Be Choosy about Fonts

Investor Guy Kawasaki has seen hundreds of presentations from people looking for funding. He has this advice on slide design:

> *The majority of the presentations that I see have text in a ten-point font. As much text as possible is jammed into the slide, and then the presenter reads it. However, as soon as the audience figures out that you're reading the text, it reads ahead of you because it can read faster than you can speak. The result is that you and the audience are out of synch. The reason people use a small font is twofold: first, they don't know their material well enough; second, they think that more text is more convincing. Total bozosity. Force yourself to use no font smaller than thirty points.*[36]

We agree with this advice. Slides filled with tiny text truly are total bozosity (in other words, do something a bozo would do).

Here are some tips for using fonts:

Use a sans serif typeface. Fonts are divided into two groups: serif (e.g., Times New Roman and Garamond) and sans serif (Arial, Calibri, Helvetica). Serif fonts look more formal and sans serif look more modern, conversational, and informal. It's easier for most people to read sans serif type because it's clear and free of fancy effects, as this illustration demonstrates:

"Kill the frills and get to the point."
—EDWARD O. TUFTE

Sans Serif	Serif
Total Bozosity (Arial 32)	Total Bozosity (Times New Roman 32)

Go big on font size. In general, use a 36- to 44-point font for titles and a 32-point font for main text. Use no more than two fonts in a presentation.

Check readability. It's surprising how often presenters use fonts that are too small to be read—or too fancy. Obviously, you should choose a font and font size that everyone in the room can read. Check to see if you can read the slide from the back of the room without squinting.

SIMPLICITY

When some years ago the U.S. space shuttle *Columbia* was destroyed in flight, a Yale professor of visual design, Edward O. Tufte, startled everyone with his explanation for the disaster.

Tufte was looking at the PowerPoint presentations given to NASA officials in the weeks before the disaster. One particular slide caught his eye, and he studied it carefully. He concluded that the slide contained crucial information that might have prevented the accident, but

> "Find out the age of the oldest person in your audience and divide by two. That's your optimal font size."
> —GUY KAWASAKI

the information "had been shunted to the bottom of a typically cluttered PowerPoint slide."[37]

It turned out that Professor Tufte was right, as the accident investigators said in their official report: "It is easy to understand how a senior manager might read this PowerPoint slide and not realize that it addresses a life-threatening situation."[38]

> "Perfection is finally attained not when there is no longer anything to add, but when there is no longer anything to take away."
> —ANTOINE DE SAINT-EXUPÉRY

Too often presentations are weak and even useless because they get so complicated and cluttered. Complexity is at the heart of a bad presentation. "Clutter" is a top reason why people hate PowerPoint presentations.

Go for simplicity. It's such a simple principle. Everybody wants you to keep it simple.

So why don't you keep it simple?

"Through the years, being called 'simple' was never a plus," says advertising legend Jack Trout. "It meant you were stupid, gullible, or feeble-minded. It's no wonder that people fear being simple." But when you're trying to connect with your audience, he says, "complexity is not to be admired. It's to be avoided."[39]

- Eliminate visual clutter
- Keep text to a minimum
- Limit builds and transitions

Eliminate Visual Clutter

Use one idea per slide.

Use special effects rarely and only for emphasis. Flashy elements clutter your slides and draw focus from your message. If your audience has to watch an arrow zigzag across the screen, make sure that arrow is going somewhere *very* important. Fancy animated effects are more likely to irritate than to charm a business audience.

Don't junk up your slides. Generic clip art is tacky and detracts from the impression you want to make. Don't include random photos "just to add interest." Cut frames, boxes, grids, and shadowing—this stuff just crowds the slide.

Keep Text to a Minimum

Don't put big blocks of text in your slides. If you want your audience to understand the message, turn this text slide into a simple chart (see second graphic on the next page).

Eliminate blocks of text or communicate the message in some simpler way—a graph, a chart, a picture. Edward O. Tufte says, "Good design brings *absolute attention* to data." Cut anything that distracts your audience from the data that will shift their paradigm.

>> design

Don't do this:

> The annual planning process usually begins with the creation of a master plan for the year focused on a large number of goals or objectives. Then, each objective is broken down into initiatives by division, and then into unit projects with their milestones, tasks and sub-tasks that must be accomplished over the coming months for the plan to succeed. The deeper the planning process goes, the more complex the plan becomes.

Do this:

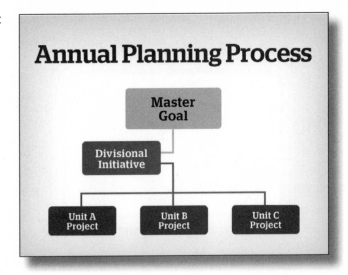

Limit Builds and Transitions

Animate text only if it will help you make your point. Don't use it "to add interest." For busy people trying to connect with your message, animations are usually just annoying frills. Use builds to reveal information as it's needed. Don't use fancy transitions between slides—we're not amused by your transitions that fly, wipe, or weep little stars.

Don't Get Too Simple

Of course, there is such a thing as "too simple." A picture may be worth a thousand words, but not if it takes a thousand words to explain it. Often we leave things out of graphs and charts that the audience needs in order to understand them.

For example, the slide on page 134 came from a presenter who was trying to sell a food supplement that would increase the "compound-G" levels in your blood (with supposedly amazing results). The increase looks impressive, doesn't it? And so simple!

But nobody could draw a meaningful conclusion from this graph—too much information is missing. What are the units on the vertical axis? Milliliters, maybe? What is a safe level of compound-G in the bloodstream? What is a "normal" level? How does an increase in compound-G correlate to the health benefits that are claimed for it?

When we pointed these problems out to the salesman, he nearly cried. "I spent $10,000 on that slide," he said.

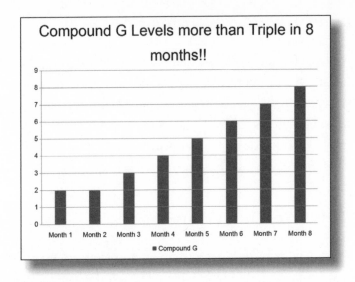

Then he brightened up. "But maybe people won't notice those things are missing."

And that's too often the problem with data presentations. If they're *too* simple, they can be misleading—sometimes deliberately so.

For visuals, the job to be done is to provide the right amount of information to shift a paradigm—no more, no less.

> "For most presenters, the notes, visual aids (usually slides), and the documents they leave behind are one and the same thing. They are not!"
> —WAHYD VANNONI

CREATE EFFECTIVE NOTES AND HANDOUTS

Now that we have developed the visual presentation for the audience, let's look at what visual tools we as presenters will use to keep us on track and help us avoid reading the PowerPoints.

First, if you need notes, go ahead and use them. There's nothing wrong with a few note cards in your hand; they give you confidence and make a serious impression. Cards or paper are fine as long as you talk to the audience and not the cards.

You can also use the Presentation Planner tool from this book as a quick reference. Fill it out to develop your message and then hold it in your hand to deliver it.

PowerPoint Presenter View is a great way to see your notes on your own screen as well as the information coming up next. Why is it important to be able to see the next slide? It helps you keep the flow going.

If your slides are simple and you feel like people need more information than you can give in the presentation, you can always create handouts to flesh out your message. See page 136 for an example of information that would be appropriate as a handout but not as a slide.

See page 136 for an example

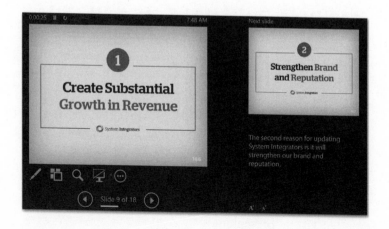

SALES ANALYSIS: 2009–2013

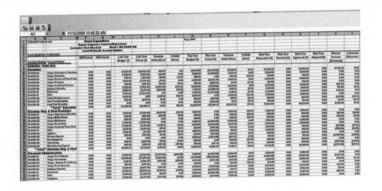

Our advice is not to distribute handouts before your presentation, because listeners will tend to focus on the paper in their hands rather than on you. Pass them out only when they become relevant or after the presentation is over.

HANDLING VISUALS IN A VIRTUAL PRESENTATION

When giving a virtual presentation, you've got to show impactful visuals to keep the participants' eyes on their screens with you and not on their email. If you don't keep them visually engaged when you're in the room with them, they might stay anyway; but if you're giving a web presentation, they might just walk away.

Here's a checklist for handling visuals during a webinar or other virtual presentation:

Make a Visual Human Connection to Your Audience

- Turn the webcam on at the start of the presentation to let the audience meet you. Turn it off after a few seconds to avoid an unnecessary distraction.

- Post your name and a picture of yourself to connect personally with the audience. Consider posting your credentials.

- Dress with the webcam in mind. Wear pastel colors; they broadcast better. Avoid striped, checked, or patterned clothing.

- Keep your background free of distractions.

Add Special Slides for a Virtual Presentation

- Add more slides than you would for an in-person presentation. Because the slides *are* the presentation, keep them moving. A rule of thumb is at least one or two slides per minute.

- Add a logistics slide up front so people know how to interact with you—by teleconference, chat, Skype, whatever.

- Show an overview slide so people know what's coming (your three key points). Show the slide again when you shift from one point to another so viewers stay oriented.

- Add a Q&A slide to signal when you're ready to take questions.

» design

- Add a concluding slide—a call for action, a request for follow-up, a next step—so viewers know the presentation is over.

Test Builds in Your Platform

- Be sure the slides can be viewed easily on any monitor. To test readability, print the slides nine to a page. If the slides are unreadable to you, they will be unreadable to the audience.

- Test any slide that builds. Builds might not work on all platforms.

- If necessary, split bulleted text across multiple slides. Consider using graphics instead of bullets.

- Try not to zoom around too much (if you're using Prezi presentation software, which has movement built in, this could be a real problem).

Interact with Your Visuals

- Use the platform's highlighting or shape tools occasionally to keep the audience's attention.

- Use the visuals to prompt discussion: "What do you see in this picture? What is this graph telling us? What do you make of that trend line?"

››› *Practice Idea*

- Select a key point from your presentation planner. Sketch a visual that would support that point with emotional impact.

- Now find a person or a pet or a wall to interact with. Use your visual to explain your point.

- How did that go? Can you make the visual more impactful? Could you design it better? Simplify it?

- Now try explaining the visual again.

- How did that go? Did you notice differences between the first and second trial?

- Create more visuals to support other key points. Then repeat this activity until you're satisfied.

- Use this checklist to ensure that your visuals are impactful:
  - ☐ Use relevant images
  - ☐ Provide visual variety
  - ☐ Use high-quality images
  - ☐ Apply a visual theme
  - ☐ Use color to create interest
  - ☐ Be choosy about fonts
  - ☐ Eliminate visual clutter
  - ☐ Keep text to a minimum
  - ☐ Limit builds and transitions

TO SUM UP ⊙

Not only do you need to have a strong verbal message, but to really connect, you must support what you say with high-quality, interesting visuals. What people see might have more impact on how they feel than anything you say.

Impactful visuals answer the "so what?" question that is on the mind of everyone in your audience.

Visuals are a very subjective topic. People have different tastes and requirements. You might say, "But I don't like a lot of graphics." Use colors and shapes instead.

"Graphics make the file size huge." Compress the file before sending, or send it through a file-sharing service.

"My audience expects me to show the spreadsheet." Put the spreadsheet in a handout. You can give an effective presentation if you follow the design guidelines in this chapter.

Good design is just good service. In the end, your job is to serve people well by getting them the information that will shift a paradigm (Know), which will motivate them (Feel) to change their behavior (Do).

You've already developed a powerful message according to the principles that help people learn and remember. Now you've created supporting visuals that are impactful, well designed, and simple. Let's move on to our last step: delivering all of that with excellence.

CHAPTER 4

Deliver with Excellence

EVERYBODY LOVED **KIP, THE FULFILLMENT** guy. It's true he talked too loud sometimes, and his enthusiasm could wear on you, but his joy in life was impossible to dislike. He could almost make you care about warehouses and supply chains because *he* cared so much.

Amita, the marketing director, was also loved and respected, but her personality was the reverse of Kip's. Quiet, introspective, and thoughtful, she oozed integrity and competence, along with a little spark of humor.

Both Kip and Amita were excellent presenters even though they were total opposites. When Kip stood to talk, he charmed you with his energy; when Amita stood to talk, she impressed you with her authenticity, so you connected to her.

Too many of us believe we can't be good presenters because our personalities get in the way. We think if you're shy or nervous or introverted, you can't get your point across in the midst of the extroverts. You might say, "I get too nervous, I can't deal with all those people looking at me, I blank out." But the fact is, *introverts can be the most persuasive of all,* whether in a one-on-one situation or a presentation in front of a hundred people.

You might lack the self-confidence of a Kip who loves to be in front of people, but that doesn't mean you can't *deliver with excellence,* the third requirement for connecting with your audience. You don't have to turn into a slick, suave speaker. Everyone has a different style, and that includes you.

"Learn to speak what you feel, and act what you speak."
—SATHYA SAI BABA

But regardless of your style, you can't deliver with excellence if the person the audience sees and the message they hear don't line up. Your body language and tone of voice must match your words. This is called the principle of alignment.

What is your first impression of the woman in this photo?

Obviously, this is one confused woman. Her words say one thing, but her body language says the opposite. She is, as we say, "misaligned with her message."

Now that you've worked so hard on a powerful message and impactful visuals, it would be a shame to lose your connection with your audience because you're misaligned with your message.

Here's a formula for getting aligned to your message and engaging the audience:

- Master the "first and ongoing impression"
- Deliver visuals effectively
- Manage good and bad stress
- Handle questions and group dynamics effectively

MASTER THE FIRST AND ONGOING IMPRESSION

First impressions stick with you. It can be done, but it's very difficult to recover from a bad first impression. People form their first impressions really fast—in about 39 milliseconds.[40] Because human brains are designed to smell out a threat, your audience immediately starts assessing this new person coming at them—*you*.

You're subject to what brain scientists call "the amygdala hijack."[41] The amygdala is a part of your brain that doesn't think; it just reacts emotionally to new things. In milliseconds, your audience forms an impression of you—are you a threat? A competitor? A resource? An ally? A potential mate?

You can't stop the amygdala hijack. When you stand up to give a presentation, the brains of your audience will be hijacked the instant they see you, and if they don't like what they see you're going to be fighting uphill from that point on. Their brains respond to subtle cues you give them, and they will decide in an instant whether to join your team or look for the eject button on their seats.

"Be yourself, but carefully."
—LISA ROSH

However, you can make the amygdala hijack work for you instead of against you. You do that by controlling as much as you can the first impression you give. You align your body language and voice with the message you are trying to get across. Here's how:

- Look appropriate and professional.

- Use your eyes to connect with the audience.
- Let your face express energy and enthusiasm.
- Use gestures to support your message.
- Use movement to support your message.
- Ensure your voice connects with everyone in the room.

Professional Appearance

Your appearance—clothes, grooming, wacky tattoo—creates an impression before you say your first word. The basic rule here is to clean yourself up, dress just a little better than your audience, and stand up straight. Remember, this is all about connecting with them.

A professional appearance doesn't mean wearing a three-piece suit. That may be totally out of place when you're talking to people in jeans and sneakers. Nor does it mean you should wear jeans and sneakers, but by looking too "professional" you could end up disconnecting from this group. You lose your credibility from the word go.

Your clothes and hair should be clean and well groomed. Makeup and jewelry should be tasteful. If you don't expect people with nose rings in your audience, then you should probably leave yours home. Also, consider what signals your tattoos may be sending if they're visible to the audience. Again, it may be just the thing for people who identify tattoos with creativity, whereas older people may associate tattoos with prison. Think about what they're wearing and align your appearance with theirs. If you don't know in advance, ask.

>>> deliver

No matter what you're wearing, you can blow it with not-so-great posture. Don't show up in a beautiful suit, with great hair and makeup and high heels, only to slouch and slump. That body language makes you look sad and small. Not a great first impression.

So think about your posture. Stand up against a wall, put your heels against the wall and then stretch your shoulder blades back until they also touch the wall. Then pull your stomach muscles in so the small of your back touches the wall. Maintain that position and walk away from the wall. This is good presentation posture.

"I don't mind making jokes, but I don't want to look like one."
—MARILYN MONROE

How does it feel? Like there's a stick running up your back? Good. You're much closer to correct posture this way. Keep practicing to strengthen the muscles that hold you up and you will find over time you will be "standing taller." And you'll connect better with your audience.

Have you ever been in a situation where someone's appearance hurt his or her ability to connect with people? Think about how that made you feel. Did their appearance hinder you from buying in to the dialogue or presentation? How did it affect their credibility with you?

What about your "virtual" appearance in an online presentation? As we said earlier, use that webcam to create the "human moment." Don't be in your pajamas when the webcam comes on. Interact virtually as if you were face to face and voice to voice.

What do *you* need to work on?

Confident Eye Contact

This is a hard fact for people who tend to look away when someone looks them in the eye, but eye contact creates an instant emotional connection. If you're not prepared, or too busy looking at your notes or your phone or your PowerPoint, then you're not connecting eye to eye with the audience. Neurology writer Erin Falconer says, "Eye contact is commonly considered a sign of self-confidence and a means for emotional connection."[42]

Good eye contact is the "emotional handshake" you give your audience.

Your eyes move faster than any other part of your body. The eyes can move 900 degrees of the compass per second, and that can work against you.[43]

Flickering or darting eye movements make you look nervous, so you should practice looking people in the eye steadily for just a few seconds before moving on to someone else. (Don't overdo it—people get nervous if you look in their eyes for more than about three seconds.)

There is no universal rule for eye contact across cultures. In Asia, for example, five seconds of eye contact is too much. In the West, a lack of eye contact makes you look shifty, insecure, or even rude (think of the server who avoids your eyes at a restaurant). Be sensitive to the culture when it comes to making eye contact.

When people comment or ask you a question, look at them. Looking away signals that you're not interested or you want to avoid the question.

Here's the funny thing about eye contact: Good eye contact is an energizer. When you are in front of an audience, sometimes you will find one or two people in the room who totally connect with you. You see shining, bright eyes riveted on you. And it gives *you* energy. And you go back to the well over and over; it makes you feel like you are doing a great job, which you probably are. But you might be ignoring the rest of the room! If you connect emotionally only with two individuals, you disconnect from the ten other people in the room.

> "One of the key elements of what is called 'social skills training' is getting just the right amount of eye contact. Too little and we come across as shy and awkward; too much and we seem rude."
> —GLEN WILSON

Sometimes we do this with whole sections of a room. We might inadvertently ignore the left side of the room while we focus on the right side. The left-side people may not even consciously think, "Why won't he look at me?" But there will be a subconscious disconnect.

Think about it. How do you feel when you walk into a room and no one greets you or even notices you're there? That's how your audience feels if you don't connect with them *with your eyes.*

When you are presenting virtually, needless to say, eye contact is essential on the webcam. Do *not* bury yourself in your notes. Remember to look at the camera, not just the screen. If you look only at the screen, it will appear that you're looking down and not into the eyes of the audience.

Expressive Face

Be aware of your facial expressions. What you radiate, the audience will radiate back to you.

You can tell when the audience is engaged because they will mirror your facial expressions. Wide eyes reflect wide eyes. Smiles beget smiles. The brain connects with and imitates what it sees because of mirror neurons, "a type of brain cell that responds equally when we perform an action and when we witness someone else perform the same action."[44]

Culture doesn't make much difference here. Your audience will interpret your facial expressions (see the following picture) the same way no matter where you are presenting in the world. Research shows that facial expressions, unlike the length of eye contact, are universal: "The discrete emotions of anger, contempt, disgust, fear, happiness, sadness, and surprise are manifested via expressions on the face . . . universally expressed and recognized regardless of culture, race, ethnicity, gender, age, or religion." This appears to be so because "muscle groups responsible for facial expressions of emotion have direct linkage to subcortical areas of the brain responsible for involuntary basic human actions."[45]

> "Don't rush to design your face to look beautiful, attractive, and charming. Rather, be quicker to decorate your mind to appear as goal-oriented, passion-embedded, and action-driven."
> —ISRAELMORE AYIVOR

So it doesn't matter if you're in Nepal or Nebraska—your facial expressions say the same things.

If you look sad, your audience might start feeling sad without being conscious of it. If you're tense and nervous, they will get tense and nervous and not even know why. Your audience will mirror your emotions and moods.

Joy Surprise Sadness Anger Fear Disgust Contempt

That's why you've got to be connected to your message. You've got to believe—and *really* believe—that if you accomplish your purpose it will make a difference. If you aren't passionate about your message—connected with it—then it will show up on your face. So what happens if your face is even a little indifferent, sad, or nervous? The audience will mirror that same emotion and your job won't get done.

Most of your listeners will be able to tell if you are faking emotions. Psychologists distinguish between real and fake smiles this way: "The skin between the eyebrows and the upper eyelid will move slightly down in the genuine smile and will not move in the social or false smile."[46] You don't have to fake it. If you genuinely believe in what you are trying to accomplish with this audience, your smiles will be authentic.

Sometimes clients tell us that they don't agree with the message they're supposed to present—that it's coming "down from above" and they don't really believe in it. This is a real concern. Some messages are downright painful, but even if you don't like them, you're responsible for promoting them. How can you be authentic while doing so?

Look deeper for your connection to the message. Why was the change made? Be empathic with the people who made the change—are you sensitive to those reasons? Can you be candid yet professional enough to move forward and work for the best possible result?

> "A good face is a letter of recommendation."
> —HENRY FIELDING

>>> deliver

One of our consultants was working with a group in Sweden who didn't like this stuff about nonverbal behaviors. They believed that working on their posture, their facial expressions, and so forth was "play-acting" and "artificial." "We want to be authentic," they said. "We don't want to be actors on a stage pretending to be excited about something when we are not."

Our consultant wasn't sure what to say about that. On one hand, he thought their concern was naïve; on the other, he didn't want to give them the idea that they shouldn't "be themselves." He didn't want to teach anyone to be a fake.

The experience caused him a lot of thought. He reflected on a time when he went into a retail store to buy a shirt. The salesperson he talked to obviously disliked her job. Her long hair covered her nervous face, her voice was low and hard to hear, and she lounged against the wall showing all the obvious signs of impatience—sighing loudly and checking her phone every few seconds as she texted her friends.

Then he knew how to answer his Swedish group.

"It's true that the salesperson was being authentic in her dislike of her job. But she was not being true to the *principle* of good service. As an employee of that business and even as a fellow human being, she should be compelled to greet the customer courteously, show real concern for meeting the customer's need, and give the customer her best attention.

> "Service is not something you do. It's something you are."
> —STELLA PAYTON

"A good presentation is just good service. Your listeners are your customers. How are you going to serve them? Courteously, attentively, showing real concern for their needs? Or are you going to be some *version* of yourself that treats them with indifference? Are you going to let your own feeling of insecurity or philosophical disagreement be more important to you than giving people what they need?"

You're not being a phony when you give people good service, and that includes standing up straight, looking people in the eye, speaking clearly, and having a smile on your face.

Think about your last great vacation. Imagine you are still on that vacation. Now, describe it to another person. Let your imagination and heart go. Is your voice filled with emotion? Are you using your hands to describe the beautiful mountains you skied on or the beach you relaxed on? Do you feel energized? Do you feel like moving a bit as you are talking? The more "connected to the message" you are, the more passionate and purposeful you are, the more naturally the right body language and vocals come.

You only look "phony" if you're not connected to your message and don't feel the need to serve your audience well. If you have no passion or empathy for the people you are speaking to, and no belief in what you are saying, then you're just acting the part. As we said earlier, always look for the connection of your message to the mission and vision of the organization. This will go a long way toward raising your level of purpose and passion for the message and providing you the empathy you need to deliver a tough message.

>>> deliver

If you're not sure how you'll come across, practice in front of a mirror or a webcam to reveal your facial expressions. Practice showing that you care about your audience, that your facial expressions and eye contact communicate empathy for them. That human connection goes a long way in helping people trust you and your message.

"Be still when you have nothing to say; when genuine passion moves you, say what you've got to say, and say it hot."
—D. H. LAWRENCE

Your face reveals your character and your principles, and as we said in the beginning of this book, your credibility comes from the inside out. You can be trusted to tell the truth, to talk straight, to be transparent about your agenda, and to know your subject. You show *one face*, and it's a real face.

Meaningful Gestures

Many times we position ourselves "naturally," only to find that those positions may not be the best way to convey our message to the audience. Let's consider a few stances. Why are the gestures pictured on page 157 generally inappropriate for a presenter?

You might fold your arms because you get cold, but people watching you get a different message: With your arms folded, you look either forced or too casual. You might clasp your hands behind you to keep from gesturing too much, but with your hands behind your back, you look like you

have something to hide. So you might fold them in front. But alas, now you look vulnerable or nervous.

Remember when you talked about your great vacation? What did you notice about your gestures? How did your gestures relate to your message? What did they communicate to the audience?

When you're excited and passionate about your message, it takes away some nervousness, and you naturally want to gesture to make your points. Often you gesture without realizing it. Just make sure that your gestures add impact to your message instead of detracting from it. Sometimes we hear people say that they "use their hands too much."

> "Confidence is like a dragon where, for every head cut off, two more grow back."
> —CRISS JAMI

Maybe they do, maybe not. Maybe they're just passionate people, which can be a real plus.

STANDING PRESENTATIONS

Here are some tips for a stand-up presentation:

- Start with your hands by your side, elbows slightly away from your body, feet planted about shoulder width apart. This is a very natural, balanced position. Remember to keep good posture.

- Use wide, expansive gestures. They go beyond the frame of your body. They radiate your passion, your emotion, and your point.

- Gesture toward the audience with an open hand, palm up. Why? Because an open hand communicates welcome, a desire to be received, while a closed hand is a negative sign in most cultures.

- Use symbolic gestures to communicate numbers. Go big if the numbers are big. If you have three points, use your fingers to mark them off. Just don't point them at the audience.

- Vary your gestures. If you typically gesture with your right hand, try to use your left as well.

The best default gestures are to have your hands at your side or hold them in front with one hand "holding the remote control." Make your gestures natural and connect them with your message.

SITTING PRESENTATIONS

Here are some tips for a sitting presentation:

- Sit on the front half of the chair with your feet planted firmly on the floor to enhance your posture.

- Rest your hands on top of the table and gesture frequently to emphasize your points.

- Keep your chin up and smile as you make eye contact with everyone at the table. Work on maintaining eye contact throughout the presentation.

- Use your audience's names when providing examples or when asking questions. This will help regain their attention and will allow for more eye contact.

- When answering a question, don't look only at the questioner. Make eye contact with everyone as you give your answer.

- Work on your vocal delivery (inflection, projection, etc.), especially when your audience is looking at visual aids such as handouts or PowerPoint slides. Use pauses for emphasis.

>>> deliver

- Don't put your hands under the table, don't fold your arms, don't lean on your elbows, and don't rest your chin on your hand.

MEALTIME PRESENTATIONS

If you're called upon to give a presentation while people are eating, there are a couple of key things to keep in mind:

- The best thing you can do while people are eating is to maintain a strong, emotive voice. (You're competing with glasses clinking and servers moving around.)
- Show high competence and a well-structured, compelling message. You will be amazed as people quietly put their forks down, because their brains are choosing to tune in on your stuff!

If your talk is a brown-bag lunch meeting, where you're all sitting and eating in a smaller, more intimate setting, also see the "Sitting Presentations" tips.

When you are doing a virtual presentation or just talking online, don't for one second think your gestures don't count. Even if your audience can't see you, use gestures to generate the passion for your subject that will drive energy into your voice.

Purposeful Movement

One of our consultants tells this story:

"Everybody in my client's firm was excited to meet the new CEO. They had all heard about the man's financial expertise and his considerable accounting background. He looked confident, even handsome as he introduced himself and started his first speech to the company.

"Then something strange happened. First one foot moved, then the other, then the first one again. The pattern repeated. Soon he was making triangles on the floor, as if he were doing a quick waltz to silent music—1, 2, 3—1, 2, 3—1, 2, 3 . . . By the end of the presentation everyone was in a trance. Nobody heard what he said, the nervous dance he did was so fascinating. That CEO was gone in six months. He had lost the confidence of the whole company in those first few minutes."

Nervous people move randomly or get into some distracting pattern of movement like this poor CEO, while purposeful movement guides the eye and demands attention. Ever see someone pacing back and forth so you feel like you're at a tennis match? Can you concentrate on the message while the presenter paces, twitches, scratches, or yanks at his clothes?

Again, connecting with people requires credibility, and you'll lose it if you don't control these things.

So how does your movement benefit the audience? It can keep the audience engaged when done purposefully. If you move closer to the audience (not *too* close, please), they will connect better with you. Move around to different audience members—don't stand by the same people all the time. Again, the audience will subconsciously feel that you're not serving them but just the people "over there."

How does movement benefit you? It actually releases nervous energy and makes you feel more connected with the audience.

MOVEMENT DON'TS

Here are some movements to watch out for. Which of these is a challenge for you?

- Entering reluctantly. When you appear a little frightened, there goes your first impression.

- Standing behind a desk or podium. This is a barrier that breaks the human connection. If you can escape this setup, do.

- Invading your audience's space. There are some cultural variations to this, but getting closer than about 18 inches in the United States makes people nervous.

- Rocking or swaying. This just plain makes people dizzy and distracted.

- Pacing randomly or back and forth. This translates as nervousness.

- Standing in one spot for too long. Your listeners' attention trails off. You need to keep their eyes and minds engaged through movement.

MOVEMENT DOS

Here are some ways to make movement work for you:

- Enter with a brisk step and smile at the audience as you enter. Show your confidence even if you are a little nervous inside.
- Remove barriers between you and the audience. Even if there is a podium or lectern, stand beside it to avoid the barrier.
- Stay at an appropriate distance from audience members. By how much varies by culture, so know your audience and position yourself accordingly.
- Position your feet shoulder width apart.
- Distribute your weight evenly on the balls of your feet.
- Plant yourself for several sentences and then move.
- Move to signal a new point or topic.
- If you notice audience members losing interest, move toward them.

The key thing to remember is that you want to move with a purpose. If you have three points to make, make each point in a different part of the room. If you're drawing a contrast between two points, make one point on one side of the room, then say "on the other hand" and move to the other side of the room. Move to the center of the

>>> deliver

"Pause before and
after you make an
important point and
stand still. During this
pause, people think
about your words and
your message sinks
in."
—ANDRII SEDNIEV

room to start and finish your presentation.

Movement is important even in a virtual presentation. Movement translates into *action*. Create movement with surveys, polls, or interactive whiteboards to engage your audience. Also, movement helps you drive a better presentation or dialogue, so get up! Stand from time to time and (if you're in a virtual meeting) even move when you can take your hands off the keyboard to get your blood moving and your energy high.

Clear Voice

Your voice reveals your passion for your message and engages the audience.

There are five Ps to master:

- Project
- Pause
- Pitch
- Pace
- Pronounce

PROJECT

Direct your voice so you can be heard clearly everywhere in the room. Take a slow, deep breath before you begin and you'll have enough air under your voice to project it without sounding shaky or tired.

> "The right word may be effective, but no word was ever as effective as a rightly timed pause."
> —MARK TWAIN

Try projecting your voice to a person across the room as if the person were catching a ball you were throwing. This is your presentation voice. Your voice might seem too loud to you, but it isn't too loud for your audience. Even if you have a microphone, try to project your voice.

PAUSE

Silence is a great thing—don't be afraid of it. Silence between statements brings people to attention. It gives people time to think; we are not very good at just shutting up to let people absorb information. Silence emphasizes, and pausing after an important point highlights the point.

A lot of presenters are plagued by what's called "the vocal pause"—saying "uh," "like," "you know," or "um" again and again. A few vocal pauses don't matter, but constant "um"s get annoying. The brain uses these fillers to cover a search for words or ideas, so one way to avoid them is to be very much on top of your message. Another way to avoid them is to practice pausing silently as you search for words. You'll sound thoughtful instead of immature.

>>> deliver

PITCH

Vary your tone of voice. A monotonous tone of voice puts people to sleep. Practice speaking as if you were telling a terrific story to a group of friends, and you'll find that natural variation in your voice. Be aware if you tend to use "uptalk," the pattern of ending each sentence as if it were a question (it's technically known as "high-rising terminals"), that it leaves the impression that you lack confidence in yourself.

PACE

Don't speak too slowly—you'll send your audience off to their own devices. A general rule is to talk a notch faster than you would in ordinary conversation. You'll keep your audience more engaged by putting on a little speed—but don't go too far. Fast talkers lose the audience, too.

Again, culture plays a role here. If you are a fast-talking New Yorker presenting to someone in a southern American state with a more laid-back culture, you need to slow down on purpose. It works in reverse as well. A person from the South may want to speed up a little to connect with the New Yorker. This is not about mimicking others; it's about gaining common ground to stay connected.

PRONOUNCE

Say words clearly. If you tend to mumble or run words together, practice each word separately as if you were trying to be heard by someone a block away from you. "Chew" your words as if you were chewing food. Your voice is your number-one tool for virtual delivery. Imagine presenting a webcast or webinar in a low, monotone voice while you're mumbling over the phone or talking to your belly button instead of emoting to the audience on the screen.

Sometimes your only hope of keeping the audience engaged is your voice.

That's why the five Ps are crucial when you are in the virtual environment. Make sure you have a very clear phone or VoIP line so your voice is not hindered. See yourself reaching around the world to "touch" that person with your voice (don't shout, just touch well).

In our global environment English is not necessarily the primary language of your participants. Make sure you're even clearer than usual with your words. Avoid unfamiliar acronyms and especially colloquialisms. If you say "the apple doesn't fall far from the tree," many people won't get it. Using clichés and slang is a great way to *disconnect* from your audience.

Remember, the key is to succeed at creating a good first impression, then maintaining that impression. You can have a powerful message and well-designed visuals, but a poor physical impression can waste all your good work. If you practice the five principles of excellent delivery, you will connect powerfully and get the job done.

>>> deliver

"True leadership stems from individuality that is honestly and sometimes imperfectly expressed ... Leaders should strive for authenticity over perfection."
—SHERYL SANDBERG

"The more I work in this area, the more I'm coming to the view that slides are the biggest single obstacle to spoken communication ever invented."
—MAX ATKINSON

Now, after you've mastered all of these principles, you'll make the perfect impression, right?

Of course, nobody ever masters all of these principles, and even if they did, it's no guarantee their messages would be worth listening to. The principles will help you, and you should work at them; but you don't have to practice them perfectly to gain the presentation advantage. Regardless of whether or not you make eye contact with each audience member for exactly three seconds, it's your personal passion for your message that makes the difference.

DELIVER VISUALS EFFECTIVELY

You've designed impactful visuals; now you need to deliver them with excellence. It doesn't always happen that way.

What's our typical experience watching a typical business presentation by a typical businessperson? Here's what goes through our minds as things get started:

> "He's lost his remote control. Good, he found it."
> "It doesn't work."
> "Oh. He forgot to put the little receiver in his laptop. Now it works."
> "What happened? The screen went blank."
> "Uh, oh. File not found. Bad news."

"Now they're calling the help desk."
"Everybody's going for coffee. I guess I'll get some, too."

And so it goes . . .

Much of the work of effective delivery happens before you start delivering. That's where you avoid the little technical mess-up that spoils the beginning of so many business presentations. Consider what you'll do before the presentation, during it, and afterward.

Before the Presentation

No pilot would fly an airplane without going through a checklist first to make sure everything's working right. As a presenter, you need a checklist you can follow so you don't crash and burn. If you possibly can, check off each of these items well before your presentation starts.

>> deliver

Use the Right Tools

- Use a remote control to advance and black out slides.

- Use presenter view so you can see your speaker notes while presenting.

- Avoid using a laser pointer. They're hard to see and they shake a lot.

- For a virtual presentation, try to have a backup computer ready to go if yours fails. Get a very good pair of headphones and a high-quality microphone.

Develop Your Technical Knowhow

- Learn how to adjust the laptop's resolution to match the projector's resolution.

- Understand basic troubleshooting in case the equipment stops working (how to change the projector bulb, check connections, set speaker volume).

- Make friends with techies who can help you, and keep their phone numbers.

- For a virtual presentation, learn as much as you can about the platform you're using. Find out how the features work—chat, polls, surveys, and so forth.

Arrive Early to Set Up and Test Your Equipment

- Do an audiovisual run-through with remote, slides, and speakers.

- Stand at various angles around the room to make sure slides are visible and sound is audible.

- Find out where the light switches are. Try them out.

- Remember—even if everything works now, it may not work later; so stay alert and keep your techie friends close by.

- For a virtual presentation, do a thorough run-through of every feature of the platform. Ask someone to log in early, watch, and listen to you to make sure everything is working.

Prepare a Backup Plan

- Have a hard copy of your presentation available.

- Have an electronic copy on a memory stick for use with another computer in case your own computer stops working.

- Be prepared to present without visuals.

- For a virtual presentation, have backup equipment ready to go immediately in case of equipment failure.

>>> deliver

During the Presentation

Here's what goes through our minds once things get started
and the presentation is actually under way:

> *"I can't see. He's standing right in front of me."*
>
> *"I wish he'd leave the slides up a little longer so I could
> figure them out."*
>
> *"He's got the wrong slide up."*
>
> *"I guess I'll read the handout."*
>
> *"Why is he leaving that slide up so long? He's not talk-
> ing about that anymore."*
>
> *"It sure is nice and cozy and dark in here . . . I'll just
> close my eyes for a second . . ."*

Here are more checklist items to help you avoid these
problems:

Help Your Audience Members See and Hear

- Avoid standing in the projector light and
  blocking the view.

- When possible, place the screen at a 45-degree
  angle for better visibility.

- Keep the lights on if you can (people fall asleep
  in the dark).

Talk to Your Audience, Not to Your Slides

- Check that your visual is displaying correctly,
  then turn to the audience to speak.

- When referring to a visual, gesture with the hand closest to the visual. Maintain eye contact with the audience.

- For a virtual presentation, keep eye contact with the webcam, not with the screen.

Avoid Verbal-Visual Interference

- Let the audience digest the slide before you talk about it.

- Reveal bullets one at a time.

- Black out the visual when it's not needed.

Use PowerPoint Shortcuts

- Press F5 to start the slideshow from the beginning.

- Type a slide number and press Enter to advance to a specific slide while in slideshow mode.

- Press the B key to display a black screen; press W to display a white screen.

What about Handouts?

Here's a little quiz:

True or False?

1. You should give people handouts at the beginning of your presentation.

2. You should give people a copy of your slides at the beginning.

3. You should provide handouts after the presentation.

4. You should create a separate, data-rich document as a handout.

Answers

1. False. If you do, participants will look at the handout and pay no attention to you.

2. False. Why attend the presentation at all if they can just read through your slides themselves? You are the presentation, not your visuals. You can always email the slides to them afterward.

3. True. Handouts are best distributed at the end of your presentation. Participants interested in your presentation will want the more detailed information in a handout at the end.

4. True. Some people will want the data or the research to support what you said. Have reference materials available.

So be smart about handouts. A few handout tips:

•   Don't use your slide deck as a handout. If you've designed your slides right, *they will not stand alone.*

- Type the handout information in the Notes pane, and print in the Notes view.

- Don't distribute data-rich handouts during your presentation. Handouts draw attention away from you.

MANAGE GOOD AND BAD STRESS

Now that you have developed a powerful message and know how to deliver with excellence, it would be a crying shame if it fell apart because of your nerves.

Do you get nervous when you present? We keep hearing that most people would rather die a horrible death than speak in public. Supposedly, three quarters of us suffer from "glossophobia," an intense fear of public speaking.[47] Are you like that?

Stage fright is a common problem, and people feel it in different ways. What does it feel like to you? Sweating, shaky hands, stomach flutters, blushing or flushing, hard breathing, mental blocks, weak knees? Most people feel some of these, and some of us feel all of them. It's surprising how many world-famous performers struggle with stage fright all their lives:

> "There are two types of speakers, those that are nervous and those that are liars."
> —MARK TWAIN

"I have big, big stage fright." —Andrea Bocelli

"I'm shy, paranoid, whatever word you want to use." —Johnny Depp

"I still suffer terribly from stage fright. I get sick with fear." —Helen Mirren

"As for the stage fright, it never goes away." —Britt Ekland

"I'm very shy. In front of a crowd I don't know where to look. I look out at a big crowd and I'll find the one in the front who doesn't clap or is looking at their watch." — Barbra Streisand

One celebrity has an interesting insight about stage fright. Admitting she struggles with it, singer Stevie Nicks says, "But I wonder: is the key to that magical performance because of the fear?"

It could be. Nervousness in presentations can be both bad and good. It is of course possible to be too nervous and lose control, but the opposite is also true. Some presenters are not nervous enough.

What do we mean by "not nervous enough"?

The largest study on human stress ever done followed 1,548 people over a period of ninety years and had a startling result: "Lack of anxiety was associated with early death."[48] Apparently, some stress is good for you.

As you present, you need *some* adrenaline in your system to fill you with energy and excitement.

However, excessive stress triggers the "fight or flight response" in the instinctual part of the brain. Fighting or running is our natural reaction to stress. (We respond this way because our prehistoric ancestors had to deal with dangers like saber-toothed tigers. We are descended from the faster people—the slower ones didn't make it.) So you tense up, the blood drains from your extremities, your heart rate soars, your mouth goes dry, and you start to shake. Everything shuts down that isn't tied to sheer survival, including your higher thinking skills. Your body is getting ready to run (which is very tempting to a lot of presenters).

The high-stress reaction is great for fighting saber-toothed tigers, but not for giving presentations. According to Dr. Daniel Amen, "Too much stress can actually damage your brain and body. Stress hormones like cortisol kill cells in the hippocampus, the brain's processing center for your memory and emotions."[49] So your mind goes blank.

There is a happy place between too much stress and not enough. It's called the "Zone of Optimum Stress," and it's where you want to be.

Think of stress as a continuum: Too little leaves you complacent and preoccupied without enough energy or interest. Too much can be destructive. You perform at your peak in your Zone of Optimum Stress—in the groove, alert, thinking clearly, in control. In the zone, you're energetic but

>>> deliver

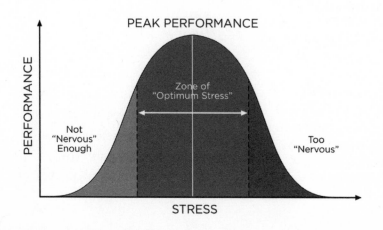

you don't quiver with nerves. So your goal as a presenter should be to *optimize the stress.*

How do you get into that optimal zone?

Prepare Well

Reading this book is part of your preparation. If you follow the guidelines in this book, you will develop a powerful message and design impactful visuals—and doing these things will give you lots of confidence.

Get Some Exercise

Your tensed-up body already wants to run—why not let it? Running or rapid walking burns up the adrenaline and cortisol that flood the bloodstream. It also uses up extra blood sugar and relaxes muscle tension. So take a brisk walk for a few minutes before you present.

> "The more you rehearse the more the fear of the unknown is removed. The more the fear is removed, the more confident you will become. As you become more confident you will feel more relaxed and your confidence will shine through."
> —GARR REYNOLDS

Meditate

Five or ten minutes of meditation can decrease cortisol, boost blood flow to the brain, and raise your progesterone levels. "Progesterone is the brain's natural Valium," says Dr. Amen. "It calms and soothes the brain. When progesterone is too low, you feel anxious, tense, and nervous."[50]

Do Breathing Exercises

When you're under stress, you breathe faster and shallower so you can fight or flee. To calm yourself, close your eyes and concentrate on taking slow, deep breaths from your stomach. You've got it right if your stomach is moving in and out instead of your chest.

Practice, Practice, Practice

If you rehearse the presentation several times, you get past the fight-or-flight mode. The more you practice, the more you create unconscious competency; and even if things go wrong, you can rely on "muscle memory" to move forward. Later we'll give you some ideas for practicing effectively.

One way to reduce stress is to get ready for the questions and group dynamics you may face during your presentation.

HANDLE QUESTIONS AND GROUP DYNAMICS EFFECTIVELY

One of our colleagues, a seasoned presenter, ran into a tough group in Paris. They were research scientists for a large drug company, and our colleague had been hired to "set them straight" on a few things. Apparently, the scientists

>> deliver

had a reputation for being, shall we say, "uncooperative with senior management" (actually, it was a lot like a street fight). On the theory that the discussion would be more "open" without them, the timid senior managers didn't want to be there.

Knowing it was going to be tough, our friend had rehearsed his presentation many times so he knew the material cold. But how to handle this hostile group?

As soon as he started the meeting, they attacked him. "Why are we here? Who's in charge? Who are you to tell us what to do? Why aren't the executives here themselves, the cowards?"

One person was a medical doctor *and* a PhD in chemical engineering (as he liked to remind everyone) with a particularly shrill voice that he used a lot. He was not about to listen to someone with lesser credentials (our friend) tell him how to do his job.

> "My answering a question and answering it to your satisfaction may be two different things."
> —WILLIAM F. BUCKLEY JR.

Our friend let them vent for about half an hour. He kept his own body language as neutral as he could make it, nodding and looking each speaker intently in the eyes. When someone grabbed the floor, he would take a step or two toward them as if the conversation were just between them. When he didn't quite follow what they were saying, he would ask, "Why do you say that?" or "Could you say that again?" He wore them out by listening to them.

When the scientists ran out of steam, he repeated in their own words what they had told him. Then he asked, "Do I have your position right?" Surprised, they agreed that he understood them thoroughly. He said, "I'm here to present some ideas that might help you work better together in this company. Are you willing to hear me out?"

It was a wild session full of hard questions, but he got through the day.

> "You never really understand a person until you consider things from his point of view ... until you climb inside of his skin and walk around in it."
> —HARPER LEE

On the morning of the second day of meetings, he was alone in the room getting prepared when the antagonistic doctor/chemical engineer came in. Our friend shrank a bit inside, but the man shook his hand and smiled. "I want to congratulate you," he said. "This has been most productive. You've done a great job moving us forward."

Sometimes audiences are difficult. If you give a high-stakes presentation, it probably won't be smooth going. Our colleague was in an unusually tough situation that you might never face, but you can learn a few important principles from it. What tips can we take from his story?

SHOW EMPATHY

Instead of trying to impose his opinion on the scientists, he started by listening with empathy. He let them vent. He didn't show agreement or disagreement; instead, he practiced Stephen R. Covey's Habit 5: Seek First to Understand, Then to Be Understood. After hearing them out, he was able to describe their point of view better than they could themselves; once they felt understood, they were a lot more willing to hear him out.

>>> deliver

You might object, "But he lost control when he let them vent for half an hour." Actually, he gained control. It was a pressure cooker in there. If he hadn't spent that time listening, the psychological pressure would have continued to build; but when they let off steam, they could relax and focus better.

SHOW RESPECT

Because our friend genuinely respects others, he didn't feel the need to "one-up" them. He listened courteously to the audience. His body language was neutral, meaning he didn't show any tangled-up emotions of his own while he was trying to understand them. Sometimes ego gets in the way, and our eyes roll or we get snarky or we bully people who are trying to bully us. On the other hand, we might feel panicky and show it. None of that is necessary.

> "If you don't stick to your values when they're being tested, they're not values—they're hobbies."
> —JON STEWART

Don't let your body language undermine you. Our friend is such a good listener, he doesn't fidget nervously or look away or check his phone; he approaches people, he looks them in the eye, and he nods respectfully as they speak. He is focused on *their* feelings, not on his own.

INVITE, DON'T COMPEL

Our friend was there to do a job, and that job was to help them, not to prove their wrongheadedness to them or to bully them into submission. When the time was right, he asked their permission to present his ideas, and they were willing to hear him because he was willing to hear them.

Don't say, "Here's what I want you to do." Say, "Let me invite you to . . ."

Don't say, "You need to do this, you need to do that." Say, "What would you think about doing this or that?"

Our friend is not just a walking bag of tricks and techniques. He is no fake. He showed empathy for those scientists because he has an understanding heart. He respected their expertise and their views. He believes in serving people, and that's why they instinctively trust him.

Handling Questions Effectively

Handling questions is another issue in group dynamics. If you've done a good job developing your message, you've already anticipated some of the tough questions and built the answers into your presentation.

But you might run into the unanticipated questions. Have you ever been in a situation where one person asks a confrontational question and others chime in, "Yeah, what about that?"

If you don't handle questions effectively, your great presentation can go downhill fast. So here are some tips for dealing with questions.

>>> deliver

EXPLAIN TO THE AUDIENCE HOW YOU WANT TO DEAL WITH QUESTIONS

Set up expectations from the first that you'll take questions at a certain time. Some people may interrupt you anyway, so be prepared for this. If it becomes a pattern, ask the person, "How would you like to proceed? In the interest of time, should we take questions now or wait until the end?"

> "When in doubt, look intelligent."
> —GARRISON KEILLOR

Listen and Understand the Question

- Make sure you hear and understand the question before answering. You know that person who finishes your sentences for you? Don't be that person.

- Just be silent and listen. Take one or two steps toward the questioner while he or she is speaking. This action helps you connect with that person and lessens the chance of a hostile question.

- Pause before responding, then restate (paraphrase) the question for everyone. A short pause communicates that you heard the question and are giving it serious thought.

Answer with the Triple S Formula

- Respond to the question using the State-Support-Summarize formula. If your response is brief (ten to twenty words), you don't need to summarize.

- Involve everyone in the answer. Don't turn the Q&A into a dialogue between you and the questioner.

- Go back to the questioner and ask if he or she is satisfied with your answer. If not, consider turning the question to the rest of the audience.

- No questions? Have a question in mind that you can raise yourself if no one asks anything.

If You Don't Know the Answer, Say So

- Don't just mumble, "I don't know." Say with confidence, "I don't know, but I'll find out." If you fake an answer, people will be able to tell, and you'll lose your credibility, so admit it when you don't know the answer.

- Pass the question to the audience if you want.

If You Face a Hostile Questioner . . .

- Practice empathy if someone strongly disagrees with you. You can also turn the question to the audience—you'll often find that audience members will defend your position.

- Say "I'm sorry, but I need to move on" if the questioner insists on an answer you can't give. Then move on.

>>> deliver

"If you hear your key points qualified, critiqued, even challenged . . . it's proof that your listeners have been so engaged by your presentation that they want the conversation to continue."
—ROLAND GRIMSHAW

Close Your Presentation after the Q&A Session

Make sure you have the last word. Restate your purpose instead of ending with someone else's question.

Stay calm, positive, and energetic throughout the Q&A session, and keep your answers short and focused on the question. No one expects you to know everything, so don't pretend that you do.

Tips for Handling Questions Online

There are a few special challenges to answering questions in an online presentation:

- Answer the questioner by name. Talk to him or her as if you were face to face. A question from an audience member is a good chance to connect personally, so make the most of it.

- If questions are coming in via chat, you could answer them on the fly, but it's not a good idea. You'll lose your concentration. It's better to get another knowledgeable person to handle chat questions.

- Don't save Q&A to the end of the presentation if you can help it. People will log off and miss your powerful close.

- Don't spend too much time with one questioner. Be brief. After the presentation, stay on the line to answer questions if possible.

››› *Practice Ideas*

The key to excellent delivery is practice.

If you can, find someone to practice on, someone you trust to listen and give you good feedback. It's hard to evaluate yourself. You need others to help you get better—family, peers, your boss. When you get feedback, be quiet and let people talk. Don't become defensive; just listen and be gracious. You don't have to accept everything they say. Here are some tips for productive practice:

- If you have several listeners, do a lightning round and get plenty of feedback. Don't stop to defend yourself—just thank each person and move on.
- Ask for verbal, one-on-one feedback.
- List questions you think you'll be asked. Ask someone to ask you those questions and practice your answers. Follow the preceding tips for handling questions.
- Don't rush through the presentation as you practice it. Do it right.
- Choose one or two points to work on. Don't get overwhelmed with feedback.

If you're practicing a virtual presentation, invite some listeners who can participate and give you feedback online. Here's a practice checklist:

Nonverbal Impression

- **Appearance:** Dress professionally for webcam and for a boost to your confidence.

››› deliver

- **Eye Contact:** Stay focused on the webcam, not on the screen.

- **Face:** Even when no one can see you, smile and be expressive. It will help convey your enthusiasm and passion for your subject.

- **Gestures:** Use them naturally to help keep your energy high.

- **Movement:** Stand from time to time to increase your energy and passion for your message.

Voice

- **Projection:** Keep the volume up.

- **Pronunciation:** Clear diction is a must for phone or VoIP (Voice over Internet Protocol).

- **Pacing:** Be aware of the audience. Speed up and slow down for variety.

- **Pitch:** You can't be monotone on VoIP or phone. Vary your tone to keep up interest. Remember, your voice is your only way to project emotion when they can't see you.

- **Pausing:** Stop talking for a moment when you want them to view a slide, think about an answer, or do an activity like a poll or a chat.

Technology

- Know the platform and its features inside out.

- Practice using the platform functions: chats, polls, slide advancing, webcam operation, audio.

- Know how to jump to a slide versus clicking forward or back to find it.

TO SUM UP ☊

Not only do you need to have a strong verbal and visual message, but to really connect, you must deliver it with excellence. In the end, *you* are the message no matter what you say or show them.

Before you open your mouth to say a word, your audience judges almost instantly the nonverbal message you send with your appearance, your face, and your body language.

And a strong voice reinforces a strong message.

Audiences are unpredictable. You can't *control* their response to your message, but you can *influence* it by preparing well and giving them empathy and respect even when they don't give it back.

These principles won't fail you. You're a well-prepared professional who genuinely wants to understand and connect with people. By definition, you win.

Conclusion

YOU MUST PAY THE PRICE to connect to people and shift their paradigms. It doesn't matter if you're standing in front of a crowd or talking one on one in the break room; it doesn't matter if you're teleconferencing with a client or running a webinar for a global audience. The same principles work to motivate change in attitudes and behavior. You must connect.

Imagine if everybody who's paid to think had the principles from this book in mind, if everyone knew how to develop a powerful message before they opened their mouths. What would it be like if everyone knew how to create "purposeful shifts in knowledge and behavior"? What if everyone practiced the principles of excellent delivery?

How many unproductive meetings would melt away? How much easier would buying in to change be? How many good ideas and innovations would emerge to move you up the ladder and your organization to the competitive edge?

This book ends where it began: It starts with you. You are your message. If you know how to *connect*—if you have passion around your message, you are seen as someone with character and competence, and your audience is engaged with you no matter how tough the subject—you've got what it takes to be a great communicator. You'll have the presentation advantage.

ABOUT THE AUTHORS

 **KORY KOGON** is FranklinCovey's Global Practice Leader for Productivity, focusing her research and content development around time, project management, and communication skills. She has coauthored *Presentation Advantage, Project Management for the Unofficial Project Manager,* and *The 5 Choices: The Path to Extraordinary Productivity.* Kory brings more than twenty-five years of expertise from frontline positions to being an executive team member. Prior to FranklinCovey, Kory spent six years as the Executive Vice President of Worldwide Operations for AlphaGraphics, Inc. She was responsible for the teams and projects that helped franchisees start up their businesses, develop staff, and reach profitability. She led the implementation of ISO 9000 globally and managed the installation of the first company-wide global learning system. In 2005, *Utah Magazine* honored Kory as one of the "Top 30 Business Women to Watch" in Utah. In 2012, Kory earned a certificate in the Foundations of NeuroLeadership from the NeuroLeadership Institute, of which she is a member.

DR. BRECK ENGLAND is Franklin-Covey's chief writer, having authored *The 3rd Alternative* with Stephen Covey and Bob Whitman, and *Great Work, Great Career* with Todd Davis and Jennifer Colosimo. In addition, Breck has taught literally thousands of business professionals how to present with excellence. Around the world, from Switzerland to Saudi Arabia, Breck has trained and coached everyone from bench scientists to road-warrior salespeople to engineers in the oil fields.

For seven years, Breck also coached hundreds of MBA students in presentation skills as adjunct professor of organizational leadership and strategy in the top-rated Marriott School of Brigham Young University.

He lives with his wife, Valerie, in the Rocky Mountains of Utah.

JULIE SCHMIDT is a Regional Practice Leader for FranklinCovey's Productivity Practice. She is a subject matter expert on *The 5 Choices to Extraordinary Productivity*, *Project Management for the Unofficial Project Manager,* and *Presentation Advantage*.

Before joining FranklinCovey, Julie spent more than twelve years with Xerox Corporation. There, she served in many roles, all with an emphasis on designing, selling, and implementing key training and consulting programs for their Fortune 1000 clients. Previous to Xerox, Julie was in the marketing industry, where she worked with organizations to develop sophisticated database marketing programs that dramatically increased their ROI.

Julie attended DePaul University and studied Industrial/Organizational Psychology. She lives in Chicago with her family, and when not working enjoys running, golfing, and spending time with family.

About FranklinCovey

FranklinCovey Co. (NYSE:FC) is a global company specializing in performance improvement. We help organizations achieve results that require a change in human behavior. Our expertise is in seven areas: leadership, execution, productivity, trust, sales performance, customer loyalty, and education. FranklinCovey clients have included 90 percent of the Fortune 100, more than 75 percent of the Fortune 500, thousands of small- and mid-sized businesses, as well as numerous government entities and educational institutions. FranklinCovey has more than forty direct and licensee offices providing professional services in over 140 countries. For more information, visit www.franklincovey.com.

IMPLEMENT **PRESENTATION ADVANTAGE**

You can increase your ability to inform and persuade by:

- Participating in an Executive Overview to see how a *Presentation Advantage*® work session would impact your team or organization.
- Connecting with a FranklinCovey client partner to diagnose presentation and communication issues and learn about the variety of work sessions that are available to meet specific needs.

Visit **www.franklincovey.com/present** for more information, or call 1-888-576-1776.

BOOST YOUR **PRODUCTIVITY**

FranklinCovey's Productivity Practice helps individuals and organizations master the three key competencies required for peak performance:

Methodically invest valuable time, attention, and energy on the highest priorities with *The 5 Choices to Extraordinary Productivity*® work session.

Complete projects on time, on budget and with the highest quality with the *Project Management Essentials for the* Unofficial *Project Manager* work session.

Powerfully inform and persuade one person or one hundred, face-to-face or virtually, with the *Presentation Advantage*® work session.

The mindsets, skillsets, and toolsets of the Productivity Suite work together, enabling knowledge workers and leaders to perform at their peak and feel more accomplished every day.

Visit **www.franklincovey.com/productivity** for more information, or call 1-888-576-1776.

ATTEND A **FREE WEBCAST**

Join a Productivity expert to learn the skills and latest neuroscience to better inform, influence, and persuade others in today's knowledge-based world. Register for a free upcoming webcast at **www.franklincovey.com/pawebcast**.

THE ULTIMATE COMPETITIVE ADVANTAGE

FranklinCovey is a global company specializing in performance improvement. We help organizations achieve results that require a change in human behavior.

Our expertise is in seven areas:

LEADERSHIP

Develops highly effective leaders who engage others to achieve results.

EXECUTION

Enables organizations to execute strategies that require a change in human behavior.

PRODUCTIVITY

Equips people to make high-value choices and execute with excellence in the midst of competing priorities.

TRUST

Builds a high-trust culture of collaboration and engagement, resulting in greater speed and lower costs.

SALES PERFORMANCE

Transforms the buyer-seller relationship by helping clients succeed.

CUSTOMER LOYALTY

Drives faster growth and improves frontline performance with accurate customer- and employee-loyalty data.

EDUCATION

Helps schools transform their performance by unleashing the greatness in every educator and student.

Notes

INTRODUCTION

[1] Cathy N. Davidson, *Now You See It: How Technology and Brain Science Will Transform Schools and Business for the 21st Century* (New York: Penguin, 2000), 200.

[2] Jonathan Safran Foer, "Commencement Address," video, 25:11, May 25, 2013, Middlebury College, http://www.middlebury.edu/studentlife/events/commencement/congrats2013.

[3] Towers-Watson, *Clear Direction in a Complex World: 2011–2012*, March 2012, http://www.towerswatson.com/en-GB/Insights/IC-Types/Survey-Research-Results/2012/03/Clear-direction-in-a-complex-world-2011-2012-change-and-communication-ROI-study-report, 5.

[4] Stephen R. Covey, *The 7 Habits of Highly Effective People* (New York: Simon & Schuster, 2013), 256–7.

CHAPTER 1

[5] Covey, *7 Habits*, 23.

[6] Stephen M. R. Covey, *The Speed of Trust: The One Thing That Changes Everything* (New York, Free Press, 2006), 30.

[7] Edelman, *2013 Edelman Trust Barometer Executive Summary*, 2013, http://www.edelman.com/trust-downloads/executive-summary/, 1.

[8] Malcolm Gladwell, "The Spin Myth," *New Yorker,* July 6, 1998, 66.

[9] "Attention Span Statistics," *Statistic Brain*, National Center for Biotechnology Information, U.S. National Library of Medicine, January 1, 2014, http://www.statisticbrain.com/attention-span-statistics/.

[10] Victoria Woollaston, "How Often Do You Check Your Phone?" *Daily Mail,* October 8, 2013, http://www.dailymail.co.uk/sciencetech/article-2449632/How-check-phone-The-average-person-does-110-times-DAY-6-seconds-evening.html.

[11] Sara Radicati, ed., and Justin Levenstein, *Email Statistics Report 2013,* April 2013, http://www.radicati.com/wp/wp-content/uploads/2013/04/Email-Statistics-Report-2013-2017-Executive-Summary.pdf, 4.

[12] Experian, *The 2013 Digital Marketing Report*, accessed February 5, 2015, http://www.experian.com/marketing-services/2013-digital-marketer-report.html.

CHAPTER 2

[13] Drake Baer, "How Screenwriting Guru Robert McKee Teaches Brands to Tell Better Stories," *Fast Company*, October 22, 2013, http://www.fastcompany.com/3020314/bottom-line/how-screenwriting-guru-robert-mckee-teaches-brands-to-tell-stories.

[14] John Medina, *Brain Rules: 12 Principles for Surviving and Thriving at Work, Home, and School* (Seattle: Pear Press, 2009), 82, 84.

[15] *Now You See It*, 9.

16 *7 Habits*, 241.

17 Henry M. Boettinger, *Moving Mountains: The Art of Letting Others See Things Your Way*, New York: Macmillan, 1989, 9.

18 *7 Habits*, 256–261.

19 Randy Olson, *Don't Be Such a Scientist: Talking Substance in an Age of Style*, Washington, DC: Island Press, 2009, 9.

20 Baer, "Screenwriting Guru Robert McKee."

21 Dan Goleman, "New Insights on the Creative Brain," *Psychology Today*, August 10, 2011, https://www.psychology today.com/blog/the-brain-and-emotional-intelligence /201108/new-insights-the-creative-brain.

22 Kurt A. Carlson and Suzanne B. Shu, "When Three Charms but Four Alarms: Identifying the Optimal Number of Claims in Persuasion Settings," *Social Science Research Network*, June 10, 2013, http://papers.ssrn.com/sol3/papers .cfm?abstract_id=2277117.

23 Diane Ackerman, *An Alchemy of Mind: The Marvel and Mystery of the Brain*, New York: Scribner, 2005, 57.

24 Annette Kujawski Taylor, s.v. "Perception," *Encyclopedia of Human Memory*, Santa Barbara, CA: ABC-CLIO, 2013, 837.

25 *Now You See It*, 27.

26 Gladwell, "The Spin Myth."

27 Antonio Damasio, "Neural Basis of Emotions," *Scholarpedia* 6, no. 3 (2011): 1804.

28 Medina, *Brain Rules*.

29 Lisa Feigenson, "Objects, Sets, and Ensembles," in *Space, Time and Number in the Brain*, eds. Stanislas Dehaene and Elizabeth Brannon, San Diego: Academic Press, 2011, 13.

30 "TedX ViaDellaConciliazione: About TED," accessed February 5, 2015, http://www.tedxviadellaconciliazione.com /about-ted.

[31] Treion Muller and Matt Murdoch, *The Webinar Manifesto: Never Design, Deliver, or Sell Lousy Webinars Again!,* West Valley City, UT: FranklinCovey, 2013, 59. (Muller and Murdoch also authored *The Learning Explosion,* FranklinCovey, 2011.)

CHAPTER 3

[32] Lionel Standing, "Learning 10,000 Pictures," *Quarterly Journal of Experimental Psychology* 25 (1973): 219.

[33] Walter Isaacson, *Steve Jobs,* New York: Simon & Schuster, 2011, 337.

[34] Shane Snow, "This Will Be the Top Business Skill of the Next 5 Years," *Contently*, February 3, 2014, http://contently.com/strategist/2014/02/03/this-will-be-the-top -business-skill-of-the-next-5-years.

[35] These terms come from Neal Ford, Matthew McCulough, and Nathaniel Schutta, *Presentation Patterns: Techniques for Crafting Better Presentations,* Indianapolis, IN: Addison-Wesley Professional, 2012.

[36] Guy Kawasaki, "The 10/20/30 Rule of PowerPoint," *How to Change the World*, December 30, 2005, http://blog.guy kawasaki.com/2005/12/the_102030_rule.html.

[37] David Feith, "Speaking Truth to PowerPoint," *The Wall Street Journal,* July 31, 2009, http://online.wsj.com/news /articles/SB20001424052970204619004574318473921093400.

[38] Ibid.

[39] Jack Trout, *The Power of Simplicity,* New York: McGraw-Hill, 2000, 5, 8.

CHAPTER 4

[40] M. Bar, M. Neta, and H. Linz, "Very First Impressions," *Emotion* 6, no. 2 (May 2006): 269.

[41] Daniel Goleman, *Emotional Intelligence*, New York: Bantam Books, 2005, 17.

[42] Erin Falconer, "Look Me in the Eyes—From Eye Contact to Fear Blindness," *Brain Blogger*, December 23, 2008, http://brainblogger.com/2008/12/23/look-me-in-the-eyes-from-eye-contact-to-fear-blindness/.

[43] Kang-chen Chen and Hye Jung Choi, "Visual Attention and Eye Movements" (paper, Donald Bren School of Information and Computer Sciences, University of California, Irvine, 2008), http://www.ics.uci.edu/~majumder/vispercep/paper08/visualattention.pdf.

[44] Lea Winerman, "The Mind's Mirror," *Monitor on Psychology* 36, no. 9 (October 2005): 48.

[45] David Matsumoto and Hyi Sung Hwang, "Reading Facial Expression of Emotion," *Psychological Science Agenda*, May 2011, 228, http://www.apa.org/science/about/psa/2011/05/facial-expressions.aspx.

[46] Ibid., 230.

[47] "Fear of Public Speaking Statistics," Statistic Brain, National Institute of Mental Health, Nov. 23, 2013. http://www.statisticbrain.com/fear-of-public-speaking-statistics.

[48] Cheryl Hamilton, ed., *Communicating for Results: A Guide for Business and the Professions*, 8th ed., Boston, MA: Thomson Wadsworth Publishing, 2008.

[49] Daniel Amen, "Foreword," in Michael Olpin and Sam Bracken, *Unwind! 7 Principles for a Stress-Free Life*, Seattle, WA: Grand Harbor Press, 2014, ix.

[50] Ibid.

INDEX